SAYING "YES"

AND "AMEN"

TO LIFE

By

W. Hamp Watson, Jr.

❖

CWP
Cambridge Way Publishing
Macon, Georgia

TO PLACE AN ORDER

THE SALES PRICE: $10.00

Proceeds from all sales will benefit The Vashti Center in Thomasville, Georgia, an agency sponsored by the South Georgia Conference of the United Methodist Church and United Methodist Women. If purchased at a United Methodist Church of the South Georgia Conference or an institution of the Conference, there will be no additional charge. Add $2.00 for a total of $12:00 including shipping and handling if ordered from W. Hamp Watson, Jr. Please make out the check to "The Vashti Center."

Cover design by Lillian Davis

Scripture references are footnoted, but reference no particular version. Most often the public domain King James Version is used.

ISBN 978-0-9746976-4-2

Saying Yes and Amen to Life

CONTENTS

INTRODUCTION

There is much happening in our world today to make us despair of life—9/11, tsunamis, hurricanes and their aftermath, crazed killers in college classes and schoolyards, and the pre-emptive and other wars spawned by sectarian violence. How do you live in a world like this and still affirm life?

In this little volume I try to address this contemporary question with ancient but timeless answers. The title comes out of an ancient text from Paul in II Corinthians 1:20, *For in Him every one of God's promises is a "Yes." For this reason it is through Him that we say the "Amen," to the glory of God.* The opening message based on this text becomes the title for the whole book, ***SAYING YES AND AMEN TO LIFE.***

How can we be positive people in such a negative world? *The Great Invitation* suggests that at least a part of the answer lies in the invitations we accept or reject in life. *The Necessary Minimum for Living* affirms that there is enough to still affirm life, in spite of all that we see around us. Down on yourself? Learn to face life with the attitude, *Just As I Am. No King but Caesar* might make us aware that life is not just our little personal pilgrimage, but that our political, national and world postures affect our continuing ability to affirm life instead of death in this world.

You get the picture. And so on through the titles in the Table of Contents that focus on our finding the best, not the worst until we know *About Amazing Grace* and find our way along *The Pathway into the Peace of God.*

It's my hope that when you finish this little book, that you will have been exposed to most of the great themes in Christian theology and practice. Perhaps it's not too much to hope that you will also feel a little better about things and that you can be one who is *Saying Yes and Amen to Life.*

DEDICATION

The proceeds from all sales for this book will go directly to the Vashti Center in Thomasville, Georgia. The Vashti Center is an agency of the South Georgia Conference of the United Methodist Church and United Methodist Women providing a number of various services to children including an emergency shelter, long-term basic care, intermediate residential treatment for emotionally disturbed children, a home for teen mothers and their infant children, marriage and family counseling, and basic education for at-risk youth who have been removed from the public education system.

My love for Vashti came from hearing Jimmy Callahan in my early ministry tell about a little girl who came with a group from Vashti to worship at First Methodist Church, Thomasville, Georgia. When time came to come to the altar for communion, the custom there was to leave an offering for the poor on the chancel rail. Others laid their bills on the rail. He watched from the choir loft as this little girl came. She carefully unraveled a handkerchief, which she had knotted, to reveal one shiny nickel that she placed on the rail before returning to her pew with a beatific expression on her face.

Later, Dr. Bill Oliver, a classmate of mine at Emory at Valdosta, became Director or CEO at Vashti, and he and his wife Naomi had some effective years of service there. Carlton and Augusta Carruth always inspired me in their constant devotion and unwavering support for Vashti. This book is dedicated to them, to the thousands who have walked in the Vashti Walkathons and to all others who have unselfishly given to support this vital ministry.

W. Hamp Watson, Jr.

Also by W. Hamp Watson, Jr.*

(1) Frederick Wilson Still Speaks – Big Words for Our Time

(2) More Big Words for Our Time
(More Frederick Wilson, some Watson)

(3) Little Stories / Big Ideas

(4) A Christmas Cornucopia

*All of the books above may be ordered by sending a check for $16.00 (covers postage also) for each book to:

W. Hamp Watson, Jr.
149 Cambridge Way
Macon, Ga. 31220-8736
478-475-1763

The amounts will be forwarded to the appropriate beneficiary listed below:
1) Benefiting the SGC Methodist Homes for Children and Youth
2) Benefiting Wesley Glen, SGC Homes for Adults With Disabilities
3) Benefiting the League of the Good Samaritan at Magnolia Manor
4) Benefiting "Miss Ella's Camp for Special People" at Epworth by the Sea

ACKNOWLEDGMENTS

*Lillian Davis, Director of Publications for the Georgia Farm Bureau Mutual Insurance Company, for designing the front and back cover.

*Donors of up front printing and production costs so that all sales may go one hundred percent to support The Vashti Center in Thomasville, Georgia, a joint ministry of the South Georgia Conference and United Methodist Women. The retired United Methodist Ministers who served as Superintendents of the Thomasville District, those who served as pastors of churches in Thomasville, and the ones who have made their home in Thomasville and have a continuing interest in this ministry have made significant contributions toward the printing cost.

*Whitehall Printing Company of Naples, Florida for a reasonable production cost and the enthusiastic cooperation of all personnel.

*Those who generously shared ideas and illustrations that are used by permission and acknowledged in the footnotes.

*The persons who appear on the pages within from whom I was unable to obtain permission in every instance, but who have shared their life and stories with me over these fifty-six years of ministry.

*Mrs. Cathy Snook, Director of Development at Vashti, and Ralph L. Comerford, President and CEO, for giving approval and enthusiastic support to this project.

W. Hamp Watson, Jr.

SAYING YES AND AMEN TO LIFE
II Corinthians 1:17-22

Have you noticed that there are positive and negative people in life? And are you like me in that you long very much to be counted more as a positive personality than as a negative person? I caught a glimpse of "Sesame Street" as I walked through the television room one morning and I stood there long enough to see two little Muppets with hard hats on that had a big YES written on the front of them. They were trying to give another hard hat with a YES written on it to the singer Judy Collins with her guitar. They wanted her to join their newly formed rock group that they had named YES. They said, "We thought about naming our group NO but that sounded so negative."

I don't think anyone wants to purposely be negative and wishy-washy and moody and depressed and down about life—always knocking things, always seeing the worst in every situation. We don't want that for ourselves because we react against that and are turned off by it when we see it in others. Some people can never be satisfied even when things are going their way. Mr. William Fawley at prayer Meeting at Bainbridge told us about the little boy and his father who were dividing up the pie when there were only two pieces left—a little piece and a big piece. The father let the little boy divide the pieces and the little boy took the big piece of pie for himself and gave the little piece of pie to his Daddy. His Daddy said, "Son, if I had been dividing the pie, I would have given you the big piece and I would have taken the little piece."

Little boy said, "Well, what you fussing about, Daddy? You got the little piece didn't you?"

You see some people are dissatisfied no matter how things turn out. They're always down about things. They say NO to life, or at best a sort of yes and no.

In his letter to the Corinthians Paul is defending himself against the charge of fickleness and untrustworthiness and as a by-product gives us some clues as to how we can become positive personalities instead of negative naggers and whiners. Listen!

"As surely as God is faithful, our word to you has not been Yes and No. For the Son of God, Jesus Christ, whom we preached among you, Silvanus, Timothy and I, was not Yes and No; but in him it is always Yes. For all the promises of God find their Yes in Him. That is why we utter the Amen through him, to the glory of God. But it is God who establishes us with you in Christ, and has commissioned us; he has put his seal upon us and given us his Spirit in our hearts as a guarantee."

Paul could say YES and AMEN to life. "Yes" the positive word and "Amen" meaning literally "So let it be." When we make our prayers and petitions we close them with Amen which is simply saying we have the confidence that that which we have prayed will come to fulfillment. So let it be! Yes and Amen—a positive way to live!

But how? How can we cease to be on and off vacillating types—up and down people? How can we stop being those so overwhelmed by our sins and errors that we think we can't change our ways? How can we avoid the moodiness that plagues our days and makes nightmares of our nights? How can our word to life cease being yes **and** no?

Like Paul, we can find proof of the promises of God in Jesus Christ. *"For all the promises of God find their yes in him."* Isaiah has God saying, *"I am he who blots out your transgressions for my own sake, and I will not remember your sins!"* Ooh! That's a tremendous promise. Though we've burdened God with our sins and wearied him with our iniquities, he'll forgive us and won't even remember our sins! Can we believe that? It's not easy to believe that just on the word of an Old Testament prophet. We know too much about ourselves and how sorry and up and down we've been. But we've found proof of this promise of God in Jesus Christ!

A young man that looked like a professional transient of the type always coming by the church for a hand-out came to the church office in Memphis, Tennessee and asked to see one of the pastors. The secretary told him they were all out but offered to send him to the centralized place where he could receive some money for food and gas. He said he didn't want that. He said he wanted forgiveness and he wanted to see one of the pastors. He hung around the church for three hours before the pastor, Doyle Masters, came in. The secretary said, "There's a young man here to see you but he's strange. He wouldn't take a handout. He says that he wants forgiveness."

Doyle said, "What's so strange about that? He's come to the right place, hasn't he, or at least what ought to be the right place?"

When the boy got to see Doyle he poured out a sordid story and asked from glazed, zombie-like eyes, "Can God forgive me for that?"

Doyle said, "Yes!"

Then he told him the story of Jesus Christ who was a friend to sinners and who laid down his life for his friends. They prayed for a while together and Doyle said, "Amen!"

The boy looked up now out of eyes not quite so glazed, where a light was dawning in the deep recesses of the brain and heart and he said, "God **can** forgive me, can't he?"

Doyle said, "Yes!"

The boy said, "I believe I can make it now."

Yes! God forgives. Amen. So let it be! Jesus is the YES to every promise of God and if you've found him you can say yes and amen to life.

And another thing: Paul says God *"has put his seal upon us and given us his Spirit in our hearts as a guarantee."* This word "Guarantee" is a translation of the Greek word "Arrabon". It meant advance payment as assurance that the full payment would be made.

When I went to buy a second hand car for my son, I didn't have the full purchase price until I could get the rest from my credit union. The man let me pay $100 that couldn't be refunded and he held the car for me until I could bring him the rest and drive off with the car. The $100 was arrabon, guarantee, and assurance that I would come back with the full payment and would participate in all the joys of driving that little car. That is I could do it until my son came and took it back with him to college.

When Paul speaks of the Spirit as an arrabon given us by God he means that the kind of life we live by the help of the Holy Spirit is the first installment of the life of heaven. It's the guarantee that the fullness of that life will some day break upon us. The gift of the Holy Spirit is God's token and pledge of still greater things to come. That's why we can say yes and amen to life. We may be down at times, but if the fruits of the Spirit like, *"love, joy, peace, patience, kindness, goodness, gentleness, faithfulness, and self-control"* are evidenced in our lives now, we know we're on the right track and can't ultimately be derailed.

> If thou but suffer god to guide thee,
> And hope in him through all thy ways
> He'll give thee strength whate'er betide thee
> And bear thee through the evil days.[1]

That Spirit or arrabon or guarantee he has given us lets us never fail nor be discouraged. We believe the promise of God that we'll know final joy, so we're joyful all along the way.

Charlie Shepard Pryor, former Lay-leader of the South Georgia Conference over at Leslie, Georgia told me a wonderful story that reaches back into the roots of his family. He had a single great-aunt who kept a hope chest only half-heartedly because time was passing and no man had asked for her hand in marriage. But a hired hand came on the place in Sumter County and worked for a while for her father. He didn't openly court her, just eyed her across the water pail or

---

[1] The United Methodist Hymnal

the dinner table where she served them, and before he left to go back to North Carolina where he had come from, he asked her to marry him. He gave her a little ring.

She'd never known him before, never knew his family, and when he left to go back to North Carolina he told her it would be some time—maybe a year or two before he came back to get her and marry her. He said he had to work out the debt on his place for a homestead, and then he'd come. So in the months that followed, his aunt filled her hope chest and sang and hummed joyously around the house. They tried to tell her that he wasn't coming back, but she'd say, "He said he would."

The months stretched into a year, then two years and she didn't hear from her fiancée. The family sadly tried to counsel with her and discourage her from having her hopes so high. Girl friends scoffed, and the father patiently, tenderly explained that he might have changed his mind or married someone else. Dozens of voices would say, "He's not coming back." But always her answer was the same as she looked at her little ring, "He said he would."

One day two and a half years later an unfamiliar carriage drove up the long lane that led to the house. From the front porch they all wondered who it might be. Finally, the former hired hand stepped out of the carriage and claimed the hand of the aunt who wore the little ring. They were married and she put her hope chest in the back, got in the carriage and went off with him to North Carolina where they raised a fine family. "He said he would." And he did. God said he would when he put his seal upon us and gave us his Spirit in our hearts as a guarantee. Don't you believe that he'll keep his promise and that you can sing YES and AMEN through life?

Then Paul says, *"But it is God who establishes us with you in Christ, and has commissioned us."* This says that we're not dependent on our own past fickle faithfulness, but we're commissioned with Christ, grounded in God. Talk about an antidote for all of life's vicissitudes! Whether things are up or down, in or out, high or low we have security in God. Paul's real defense against the charge of fickleness is not that he is wise, consistent, and skillful but that God is using him and directing his life. Only the life that God confirms and establishes is stable and reliable.

Martin Niemoller, the great Lutheran Pastor and resistance leader in Hitler's Nazi Germany, was incarcerated for three years in the prison and death-house at Dachau. He was surrounded by the stench of burning flesh as the Nazis disposed of the bodies of Jews and other enemies. He was kept in solitary confinement. When asked how he stood it, he said, "You never know how strong you are and how much you can stand until you know that God dwells in your life."

Who trusts in God's unchanging love,
Builds on the rock that naught can move.
It is God who establishes us.

Since I was about eight or nine years old I have loved and recited Sidney Lanier's poem, "The Marshes of Glynn" because my Daddy loved it so. He knew it by heart from the beginning to the end. I once drove a bus to take some older adults on a trip to Epworth-by-the-Sea and drove under those mossy oaks. The sight of those oaks made me wax eloquently saying,

Beautiful glooms, soft dusks in the noonday fire,
Wildwood privacies, closets of lone desire,
Chamber from chamber parted with wavering arras of leaves,
Cells for the passionate pleasure of prayer for the soul that grieves.

Those old folks thought their pastor had gone crazy up there driving that bus. But there's another part of that poem that I never fully understood until that trip to Epworth. It's the part that goes:

As the marsh hen secretly builds her nest on the watery sod,

Behold I will lay me ahold on the greatness of God.
Do you know how the marsh hen builds her nest? I didn't.
Mary Nell Waite in the Museum at Epworth told us. She said,
"The marsh hen weaves her nest around the deep rooted
marsh grass in such a way that when the tide comes in, the
nest rises and falls with the water." So whether the tide is in or
the tide is out, whether the tide is high or the tide is low, I
build my nest on the greatness of God whose roots reach
down to the soil, and regardless of the tide I am secure in the
greatness of God. O yeah! We can say yes and amen to life
because: We've found proof of the promises of God in Jesus
Christ. All the promises of God find their yes in Him. We
have certainty of our final, full participation in the best that
life offers because it's sealed and guaranteed by his Spirit that
we know now. And we're commissioned with Christ,
grounded in God.

As the marsh hen secretly builds her nest on the
watery sod,
Behold I will lay me ahold on the greatness of God.
I will fly in the greatness of God as the marsh hen
flies,
In the freedom that fills all the space twixt the marsh
and the skies.[2]

I will say YES and AMEN to life! Yes! And Amen!

---

[2] Sidney Lanier, native of Macon, Georgia, Baltimore 1878

THE GREAT INVITATION
Luke 14:15-24

The great invitation has been issued. Jesus tells us about it in this wonderful little story about a king who threw a great banquet. He invited a great number of people by special invitation and then when the time for the feast came he sent his servant to tell them that it was ready. Of course, Jesus here is talking about God. God has issued the invitation to come into the kingdom of God, to come under the rule of God in this life, now, and to sit down in the heavenly places for eternal feasting and fellowship. God has sent a special invitation to many people.

But in the story a strange thing happens. We'd think it was strange if we announced a Golden Wedding Celebration at Glenwood Hills with one of our famous dinners and nobody showed up. This would be unbelievable. In this parable, the unbelievable happens. Here God has issued the invitation to a great feast, eternal life, communion with God through all eternity and the invitation is turned down. All sorts of excuses are invented in apology and every imaginable loophole of escape is ingeniously devised.

One man says that he's bought a farm and has to go look at it. Anybody knows that he could eat first and look later. The farm wasn't going to run off while he was at the banquet. Another man says he has to try out a team of oxen he's just purchased as if he couldn't tie them up and try them later. Another man who looks like he has a pretty good excuse says that he just got married. But it seems to me that this would have been a golden opportunity for him. It would save him the price of at least one big meal on his honeymoon. The truth of the matter is that they just didn't want to go. They were hunting for some excuse to turn down the invitation. They didn't have any, so they just made some up.

"I cannot come to the banquet.

Don't trouble me now.

I have married a wife.
I have bought me a cow.
I have fields and commitments
That cost a pretty sum.
Pray hold me excused.
I cannot come!"[1]

They gave their excuses, but I wonder about the real reasons they turned down this invitation. Why do any of us turn down invitations? There are a lot of invitations that come to us that we don't accept. What are our reasons for turning them down.? I thought about some of the invitations that I've received that I've turned down. I thought about the reasons that I didn't go.

Sometimes I don't accept an invitation because I think there's something more important that I have to do. Back before retirement, since I led singing for revivals and preached in revivals, one year I had thirty invitations to help in revivals. I turned down all but four of them. Why, because I'm against revivals? No. It was because I thought it was more important for the pastor of a people to be with them, studying and preaching and counseling and administering the work of the church. Besides, I knew I would be out on my ear without a church to serve if I accepted that many revivals. I don't accept an invitation because I think there's something more important that I have to do.

So it was with the people of Jesus' day. He says they thought some other things were more important than entering the kingdom of God. The wealth of a farm, the power of a fine yoke of oxen, the excitement of marriage—these were all vital concerns. These were all important, but the voice of God could wait until sickness came or death summoned them. Isn't it that way today? When I served churches that had a lot of people with jobs it would take a major tragedy to make some of them miss a day of work. But a case of sniffles could keep

[1] From *Joy is Like the Rain*, Youth Musical

them home from church. We have Sunday sicknesses, most of us, but we'll be all right on Monday... at least all right enough to get back on the job.

Our physical welfare, mental welfare, family welfare and all the rest must be satisfied first, and then we might turn to respond to God's invitation. In effect we say, "God, there are some other things that we think are more important." Now, I wouldn't make church going equal to responding to God's invitation. But if somebody consistently makes other things more important than attending the services of his or her church, it at least raises the question—"Do I think that other things are more important than the rule of God on this earth?"

I also turn down invitations because I don't think I'll have any fun if I go. I remember the Wesleyan Service Guild at First Methodist Church, Griffin, Georgia, invited me to speak to them one night and I started to turn them down. I would be the only man there, and who could possibly have any fun when he's the only man in a roomful of women? I knew they wouldn't have much to eat, just a lady's sized supper, and that it would be as formal as I thought ladies meetings were. I'd have to watch whether I was using the spoon and fork in the right place or what. I like to push English peas up on my fork with my bread and I was afraid they wouldn't let me do that. Actually, I went ahead and spoke for them and they gave me two plates instead of one, and all the women were so busy talking that they didn't have any time to watch my manners, and really, I had a big time. But I didn't want to go because I was afraid I wouldn't have any fun.

People feel the same about God's call to his church and to the Kingdom's rule in one's life. They think it's a dull affair. Maybe we preachers are guilty here. They watch us. They watch us dodge controversial issues. They watch us shilly shally around. They get the idea that humankind's most final and demanding fellowship is just a flabby, respectable luncheon club affair. We preachers give the impression of being harmless little people, mild and mannerly, cautious and safe, sour and critical who couldn't possibly know anything about having a good time. God's kingdom means denying oneself, avoiding joy, pleasure and fun, they think, and for this reason many people turn down God's great invitation.

Are you also like me in that you sometimes don't accept an invitation because you think the folks don't mean it? The invitation isn't seriously issued. Their invitation isn't real. I don't blame them particularly. It's just the custom. It's a part of Southern hospitality. They issue an invitation, but they don't have any intention of actually having the occasion or of you showing up for it. I've heard my wife say, "Y'all come and eat with us... just anytime." But if the folks she was asking were to drop in at mealtime to eat, she'd drop through the floor. You have to watch these invitations. There may not be any meal there waiting for you.

When I was a single, hungry preacher, a lady said to me, "Come by and eat with me just any time." So I went by one night about suppertime. You know what we had? Rabbit food—lettuce, cabbage, and radishes... stuff like that. She happened to be an officer in the Business and Professional Women's Club. I like rabbit food sometimes, but when it's rabbit food left over from entertaining the B and PW Club the night before; I don't care too much for it.

There are people who don't respond to the invitation to the banquet of God's kingdom because they don't think the invitation is real. They don't think they'd get anything if they went. They don't believe in anything that they can't see, smell, taste, touch and feel. You have to prove the value of anything to them in dollars and cents. Things of the spirit like love, joy, peace, patience, kindness, goodness, gentleness, faithfulness and self-control are not realities to them. You see, for many people, the body cries out, "I'm near, serve me", while the soul is just a sound of silence. Earth is a hard fact while heaven is only a hope, and God hardly stands a chance alongside investments, a car, or a wedding. This is why it is that so many people sell their lives for colored glass while God offers them jewels. They don't believe in the reality of the great invitation. They don't believe in any values they can't put a dollar mark on. They don't believe there's going to be any banquet table in the king's house. They don't believe there will be any final judgment. They believe only in what they can get and hold for themselves right now.

People turn down the invitation to God's banquet because they think they have something more important to do… or they don't think they'd have a good time if they went… or they don't think the invitation is real. They don't take it seriously.

Have you guessed by now that I'm going to tell you that we ought to accept this invitation? We ought to accept it because accepting it is the most important single issue in life. Now a farm is important. The way a person makes a living is important, but we couldn't have a farm without God. The Bible says, *"The earth is the Lord's."*[2] A team of oxen or a car is important. We need a way to get around, a way to go, but what point is there is going anywhere unless *"The Lord thy God shall go with thee whithersoever thou goest?"* Marriage is important. Two are joined together, they become one and share life. But what point is there in being joined together unless your marriage is, *"What god hath joined together that no mortal can put asunder?"*[3]

And you don't think it would be any fun? We ought to accept this invitation, because it holds in it the deepest joy in life. At the close of the World War II when our great civilian army was being demobilized and the soldiers were coming back, a preacher named Theodore Maudlin said, "My wife and I were calling the other day on a young woman whose husband had been three years overseas. We sat on the porch while she was preparing some tea for us in the kitchen. We saw a young man in uniform walk toward the house and stop

---

[2] Psalm 24:1
[3] Matthew 19:6

at the gate. For a long moment he looked up at the house, then came up the steps, paid no attention to us, and walked in the door. He quietly set his duffel bag down and listened to the rattle of cups in the kitchen. Then he whistled softly an old tune, and the noise in the kitchen stopped. Then we heard her moving toward him in the hall. There they stood a few feet apart, their hands touching. No words were spoken, but all that two people could say with their eyes was said. He cleared his throat, then slowly reached down into his duffel bag and brought out a box. With superb calmness, he said, 'Darlin, here's the candy I went out to get for you.' Her eyes were filled with happiness, framed in a crystal circle of tears. But when she spoke, her calmness matched his.

She said, 'Thank you, Dear, but I think you were a long time getting it.'

Then they were in each other's arms, and we tiptoed out the gate."[4] The spiritual puts it, "I'm gonna eat at the welcome table. I'm gonna eat at the welcome table some o' these days, hallelujah. I'm gonna eat at the welcome table. I'm gonna eat at the welcome table some o' these days." Where could there be more joy than that—reunion with the Father in the Father's house?

Is this a seriously issued invitation? I don't think God's just saying, "Y'all come." This is the most seriously issued invitation of all time. I remember the night I was at the football game between Rochelle and the Fitzgerald B. Team. It was the first year Rochelle had ever fielded a team and the whole town had turned out. Day was in the car with Wade and I had the toddler, Susan, with me on the sidelines. Just before the end of the game there was a lull in interest and Johnny Laidler and I got to talking. When the B Team from another school has your team 62 to nothing there tends to be

---

[4] *Horns and Halos.* J. Wallace Hamilton, p. 159)

a lull in interest. Before I could stop her, Susan darted off in the crowd in the direction of the stands... the opposite direction from where our car was parked. I ran after her but immediately lost sight of her in the push. My heart sprang up into my throat, for just about that time the whistle blew signaling the end of the game and the mad rush for the cars started. I could see Susan being trampled underfoot, or under the wheel of a car. I started running madly through the crowd screaming at the top of my lungs, "Susan! Susan! I've lost her. Somebody help me find Susan!"

I spotted three of our babysitters, Margaret, Martha, and Boopy, and I put them to work helping me. Then I thought to climb up to the top of the stands to ask the announcer to ask everyone to stop where they were until I could find her. It took him forever to switch on the speaker to say, "Everybody hold still. A little girl has been lost. Help find Susan Watson!"

Pretty soon the word came that she was back at the car with her mother, and my heart came back down out of my throat. She had cut back through the cars, going in the opposite direction from me, and she had found our car.

Is this too far from it? I think God comes to earth personally, searching frantically through the crowds of the world's life for a lost child. The invitation to come back is sounded at the top of God's voice. So serious was the invitation that God finally called it out from a cross on top of a hill and God will never relax until every one of God's children makes it safely home.

There's an ending to the little story that Jesus told. When the invited guests refused the invitation, it may have broken the heart, but it didn't thwart the purposes of God. The banquet went on. It simply passed those by who turned down the invitation.

God has issued the great invitation. Every person is writing an answer to it. It is, "Please present my regrets", or it is, "Thank you, my Lord, I'm coming." I think I know the answer you want to give.

THE NECESSARY MINIMUM FOR LIVING[1]
Deuteronomy 29:29, Luke 13:1-5, I John 4:7-12

Things are always happening that make us raise questions about God and life: whether God is just, whether life is worth living, whether you can trust and love a god that allows such things to happen in what's supposed to be a good world that God has made. When the United Nations said that Asia's tsunami death toll could double to about 300,000 unless survivors received clean water and other basic services by the end of the week to prevent disease, we're just overwhelmed at the magnitude of such a tragedy.

When crazed killers shoot innocent children in schoolyards, we hear the explanations and cries of gratitude from those who think that God somehow preserved them, but we are dissatisfied knowing that other innocent children perished, whose families and perhaps they themselves had prayed just as hard. A few years back, why had the youth group already left the building when the Centenary Church hall collapsed in Macon? Were they more deserving than thirteen youth that were killed on a Baptist bus in the mountains? What about those who perished in 9/11? We can't imagine that they all deserved it, or come up with any ready explanations.

It was true of the people in Jesus' day. When Pilate had a bunch of Galilean Jews killed when they were in the very act of worshipping God, some people asked Jesus about it. That's political terror. That's murder, human beings killing innocent human beings. They must have also asked about natural calamities, about the eighteen upon whom the tower at Siloam fell. Because Jesus' answer comes in response to both these issues: innocent death and tragedy caused from inhumanity, and tragedy from natural calamity.

---

[1] Preached January 9, 2005 after the tsunamis in Southeast Asia

Obviously the questioners expected Jesus to come up with the conventional answer gleaned from Old Testament Wisdom literature: bad things happen because these were bad people. At least they wanted some other answer that made sense as a logical purpose that God had for it. People are still trying to come up with such answers.

My friend, Creede Hinshaw, reports that an outfit called Tornado Research is trying to discover a correlation between church attendance and tornado or lightning victims: Do tornadoes seek out non churchgoers? They asked these questions of a pastor after lightning killed one of his members: Male or female? How old? Affiliated with the church? Did the person go to church "Once a year, occasionally, regularly, or very active in church work?" Just think of the implications if they discover that tornadoes and lightning seek out the backsliders! Church pews would become full again. Offering plates would overflow. Evangelizing Bibb County and the world would be a snap. We could scare heaven into people. Maybe insurance rates for regular attendees could be reduced, too. What a revival would take place! I wish it was that easy, but Tornado Research won't have much success with its surveys. The Biblical testimony from Job to Jesus has been that tornadoes are not choosy.

A tragedy comes in a family, like the mother who interrupted my prayer after the death of her five-year-old with bulbar polio to ask, "Why did God let this happen to her?" I was crushed **with** her, sharing her grief, and silent I think. But in the next few days there were those well-meaning friends who dropped by with ready answers. Mrs. Itcud Benworse came by. So did Mr. Ujust Gottatakit. Mrs. Uwill Learnalesson dropped in. But the worst one was Mrs. Itwas Godswill. Jesus did no such shallow counseling that insulted the sufferers and maligned God.

So far as we can tell, Jesus said only about three things on the subject, none of which were in direct answer to the question. To the ones wondering about those killed by Pilate and crushed by the tower falling, he just said, *"You think they were any worse than others? I tell you no! And unless you repent, you shall all likewise perish."* That's not very comforting. He doesn't explain why. He just turns the question and makes it into a question about whether those wondering are themselves right with God. Human and natural calamities are calls to be ready and calls to repentance for all of us.

In another place he says that God, the heavenly father, *"sends his sun to shine upon the evil and the good and his rain to fall upon the just and the unjust."*[2] This seems to suggest that there is a random character to the good and bad things that happen to us in life. When his disciples ask him about whether the man born blind sinned or whether his parents sinned to cause it, Jesus said, *"It is not that the man or his parents sinned. He was born blind so that God's power might be displayed in curing him."*[3] In other words, every occasion of natural and human calamity is an occasion for God and the people of God to go to work to remedy it if at all possible.

But Jesus doesn't seem to have any interest in giving us a philosophical or theological or even logical answer as to why bad things happen to good people or what you're supposed to do about it when it does happen.

Jesus didn't give all the answers. As a good Jew he must have known the old verse from Deuteronomy 29:29, *"The secret things belong unto the Lord our God, but the things which are revealed belong unto us and to our children forever."* Ah, the secret things! When trouble comes, we look eagerly for some little ray of light, some sign in the sky. We listen for some voice to speak, some hint of what God means, and listening, we hear nothing but silence and a long lingering stillness. There'll always be mystery as to why the good suffer. But the question is, "Do we know enough to live and to affirm life and God?"

---

[2] Matthew 5:45
[3] John 9:2-3

Those things which are revealed belong unto us and to our children forever. Is there enough revealed?

This is the old question of the law of the necessary minimum, and we apply it in much of our lives. We go out to woo a bride and we might want one like the old Preacher-Philosopher Charlie Ledbetter of our Conference talked about. Somebody asked him when he was serving at Rhine, Georgia, why he hadn't married again after his wife died? He said, "Next woman I marry'll have to be as rich as Mrs. Rockefeller, as pious as Susannah Wesley and as pretty as Mae West." But most men are content with less. Does she love me? Can she cook and run a family? And, these days, "Can she earn half or more of the living?" Can she keep her mouth shut long enough for me to tell her all of **my** problems? Then I'll marry her! I know enough. This is the law of the necessary minimum.

I don't mean to be flippant about such a serious subject because there's a dark side, a tragic side, a mysterious side— much which would make us want to give up life. There's much that we don't know. But, do we know enough? Do we have the necessary minimum? *"The secret things belong unto the Lord our God, but the things which are revealed belong unto us and to our children forever."*

We **do** know enough! Here are some of the things that are revealed: Lamentations 3:33 *"God doth not willingly grieve nor afflict the children of humankind."* If anything bad happens to good people, or to anyone, God doesn't want it to. I do know enough. God is there and God is kind. God is love. John who wrote, *"God is love,"* had lived a long life. He had every reason to know the dark and the mysterious. There were plenty of "Whys?" around him. Lepers were segregated in dying communities or in isolation. Women vended their bodies for bread or were exploited as temple prostitutes. Nero boiled the Christians in oil. But John looked at it all and said, *"God is love!"*

Where did he learn it? Did he learn it from the stars? No, the stars are cold. Did he learn it from nature? No, nature speaks with two voices. Flowers can make a funeral wreath as well as a lover's bouquet. Nature is sometimes red in tooth and claw. Did he learn it from human nature? No, for there's the stench of the burning of the Jewish children in incinerators that hovers over humanity ever since Hitler. There's the horror of Hiroshima and the Hydrogen Bomb cloud, the Oklahoma City bombing by men from America, and the Twin Towers toppling by those who would kill themselves for the glory of killing Americans. From where we stand, human nature is foul.

Where did John learn it? John knew Christ and he knew he was love. He knew Jesus said, *"Those who have seen me have seen the Father"* and God is therefore love. This is a thing that is revealed. The secret things belong unto the Lord our God, but it is no secret about the love of God. We can write this down! This belongs to us and to our children forever. This is the necessary minimum.

From the beginning of time, people have pelted heaven with their prayers asking "Why?" and they have been met with a silence—the silence of God. Many have complained and turned bitter. But they have had to recognize that this was not necessary. This was their choice. Others hearing that same silence have not complained nor grown bitter. They have found it not to be a harsh silence. *"In the night of death, hope sees a star and love hears the rustle of a wing."*[4]

A popular monk in the middle ages announced that in the cathedral that evening he would preach a sermon on the love of God. The people gathered and stood in silence waiting for the service while the sunlight streamed through the beautiful windows. When the last bit of color had faded from the windows, the old monk went to the candelabrum and took a lighted candle. He walked to the life-sized crucifix, the

---

[4] Robert Ingersoll, the agnostic, at his Senator brother's funeral.

simulated body of Jesus on the cross. He held the light beneath the wounds on his feet... then his hands... then his side. Then, still without a word, he let the light shine on the thorn-crowned brow. That was his sermon. The people stood in silence and wept while the message went into each heart. Behind the darkest shadow we can see the shadow of a cross that says, "God is love." You are not alone. God suffers too. God is love! What about the things that happen that make no sense—the tragic things in life? Why is there calamity, why insanity, why cancer, why polio, why birth defects, why tsunamis? I don't know. I only know the character of our great God can be utterly trusted. God is love and cannot be false to God's nature, and I count on that. This is the necessary minimum for living. *The secret things belong unto the Lord our God, but the things which are revealed belong unto us and to our children forever.* Is that enough? Is that enough for you? I hope so!

JUST AS I AM
Psalm 40:5-7, Isaiah 55:1, I Corinthians 1:26-2:5

I would venture a guess that this song, JUST AS I AM, has been used to close more Revival services in the South than any other song in Christian hymnody. As a boy growing up in the Baxley Methodist Church I used to get so tired of it. I heard it used a hundred times in my own church and every time I ventured over across town to the Baptist Revival, there was no release there. The Baptists were singing it too. I began to ask; "Don't the preachers know any other closing hymns?" Why in the world do they have to overwork that one so much? Later, after I had hit the sawdust trail song leading and helped in many revivals, I noticed it was the same all over. The whole state of Georgia was as wild about the thing as Baxley was.

Once I was teamed with a professional evangelist and had a chance to get my question answered. I noticed that this man would use no other hymn to close a service but this one. As he made his appeal for converts to come to the altar, he invariably announced, JUST AS I AM. If no one came after the six stanzas, he would sing them over again. My arm would nearly break off from waving out JUST AS I AM.

So I asked him on our way out to a meal one day, "Why do you use that song so often?"

He answered me in a way that confirmed my suspicions about him. I had already begun to doubt his sincerity. He was worried about how the offerings were coming in and he was fearful that we'd have no converts to show for the meeting. He was self-righteous and overly pious and becoming obnoxious to me already.

He said, "Just as I am is essential to a good meeting, Son. It's a psychological tool to get converts to the altar. You've heard about the power of suggestion, haven't you? If people have something suggested to them long enough, they'll begin to think it's their own desire. This is the reason for the repetition in television commercials. They say it over and over again until the mind accepts it. Well, I sing JUST AS I AM at the close of a service and it's even better than that. It's autosuggestion. The person sings, 'Oh Lamb of God I come, Oh Lamb of God I come, Oh Lamb of God I come' until under the power of his own repetitive suggestion he turns loose that pew and comes to the altar."

Whew! That clinched it! I knew that he was a charlatan using psychological gimmicks to hoodwink people into doing what they didn't really want to do in order to make a convert record for himself, build up a reputation as a great evangelist and line his own pockets. If I had disliked the song before, I began to distrust it and class it as a gimmick that unscrupulous people who didn't belong in the ministry would use.

But I'm offering it to you, dear reader. Why this change of attitude toward JUST AS I AM? Why do I regularly use that which I once despised? It's because I discovered that that unethical evangelist was wrong. JUST AS I AM is not widely used in Christian Worship because it's a psychological gimmick or because it moves people to an altar by autosuggestion. It's widely used and loved because it suggests an attitude that's basic to life. And most of all, it suggests an attitude that's absolutely necessary for a person to have before finding new life in Christ Jesus.

For instance, JUST AS I AM relates to self-acceptance. A boy starts to school and wants to be a space scientist, but he flunks his math courses. If he can make a readjustment and accept himself with a sane estimate of his own capabilities and continue to work at what he can do, then he's learning to accept himself and face life on the basis of the healthy attitude, JUST AS I AM. A part of growing up is simply learning to be yourself—your own God-intended self with potentiality and talent as God made you. It's following the advice of the child-care person of yesteryear who often said to her charges, "Be what you is and not what you ain't, 'cause when you is what you ain't you ain't what you is." In this sense all of us have to learn to accept ourselves and face life just as we are.

Just as I am relates to how partners in marriage have to accept each other if they're to have a good marriage. They have to learn before marriage to accept each other as they are—for better for worse, for richer for poorer, in sickness and in health. Over and over I've told young people at the dating age who were beginning to get serious about the choice of their life partner, "Pick a partner with whose basic characteristics you'd be content to live all your life. Don't go into marriage on the basis that you're going to make your darling over. If he or she has some bad habits or attitudes now while dating, don't live under the delusion that you through your love will be able to get that particular thing out of him or her."

At the altar of the church we accept each other just as we are. This includes friendships, in-laws, aunts, uncles, nephews, mother and father, life-long associations, characteristics, habits, relatives and everything else about them. "The fleas come with the dog." If you can't accept all this it's usually wiser to seek out another life partner rather than to romantically think you're going to change all this later.

When I preached along this line one time a lady came up to me after the service and said, "When a young woman goes to her wedding ceremony she has her mind on three things— the aisle, the altar, and the hymn; or 'I'll alter him.'" But both partners had best think the other way and assume that they're accepting each other just as they are.

But most important of all JUST AS I AM relates not only to self-acceptance and to acceptance of partners in marriage, but it relates to God's initial acceptance of us. Sometimes youth groups have "Just as you are" parties. They'll call at an odd time during the day to invite the ones to come to the party and the rule is that those called have to come in the state of dress they were in when they answered the telephone. Of course they'd make a few exceptions—those caught below a minimum standard of decency would be allowed to put on a robe. But basically they were to come just as they were. Just as you are.

This is how God calls us to approach him in our faith. Isaiah has God saying, "Ho everyone that thirsts, come to the water. And you that have no money, come buy and eat."[1] We can come into the presence of God with no previous long-range changes in character achieved. He takes us in his care and begins working with us before we deserve it; before we can point to anything we've done or achieved that would make us worthy of God's care and concern. Without any special dress of righteousness we come—just as we are. All who are spiritually dissatisfied are summoned; those who are thirsty and hungry for God can come. They don't have to buy God's favor with any piled up accomplishments of goodness. We have it in another hymn,

"In my hands no price I bring
Simply to thy cross I cling."

This was the only requirement—humble desire. And when the Master came calling people he just said, "Come ye after me, and I will make you become fishers of people."[2] No previous condition of excellence as fishers of people was demanded. Jesus was and is in the disciple-making business. He never picked them ready-made. He was making fishers of people—Matthew, the cheating tax collector, Simon, the cowardly fisherman, Paul, a persecutor of Christians, the woman at the well that had had five husbands. He took them as they were and made them over into a gospel writer, the rock on which the church was built, a man that wrote half the New Testament, and a flaming evangel who cried out *"Come see a man who told me all that I ever did. Can this be the Christ?"*[3] The only initial requirement was their desire to follow him.

---

[1] Isaiah 55:1
[2] Mark 1:17
[3] John 4:29

And the most gracious invitation that ever fell from the lips of our Lord has no requirement in it except the admission that we are bowed down and burdened. "Come unto me, all ye that labor and are heavy-laden and I will give you rest."[4] He made the invitation to those who acknowledged their own weakness, to those who acknowledged that they had sins to be forgiven and were bowed down and burdened. Maybe this is the reason that he had so few to take him up on it back then. That may be the reason we find it so hard to take him up on it now for its demand is that we come with humble desire, admitting our own sins and weakness—just as we are. It's the only demand, but so many will not eat humble pie.

I heard John Branscomb tell about a man with one leg in Florida. He and his wife could have no children and it was difficult for them to adopt through DFACS. Because of his handicap more qualified candidates would get the child they were waiting for. But finally a doctor friend called one day and said, "Jim, come on to the hospital. I think there's a child here that you and Mary can have, if you'd like to have it."

Jim picked up Mary and rushed to the hospital. As he came up to the hospital window where the babies were shown, the doctor stopped him and said, "Jim, you may not want this child. I think I had better warn you now. The reason it's available is that it was born without one hand."

Jim pushed the doctor aside and looked through the window at the little fellow lying there and said, "All right, little fellow, you take your one hand and I'll take my one leg and we'll face this world together."

He turned to the doctor and said, "We'll take him, Doc, nub and all."

This is the way God takes us—"nub and all." He takes us just as we are and lets us grow up in his presence. Recognizing this spirit in God the Psalmist cries,

Sacrifice and offering thou didst not desire.

---

[4] Matthew 11:28

Burnt offering and sin offering hast thou not required.
Then I said, "Lo, I come."[5]

A later hymn writer took this same spirit and put it into song. Charlotte Elliott had passed through deep waters of physical and mental suffering. A friend of her family had offended her in asking her if she were a Christian, but angry as she was, she later asked him how she could come to Christ.

He said, "Just as you are, Charlotte."

So Charlotte came to her Lord just as she was—petulant, cross, and ugly spirited. Later she voiced her certainties around the phrase dear to her. And so she wrote and sang,

Just as I am, without one plea
But that thy blood was shed for me,
And that thou bidst me come to thee,
O lamb of God, I come.[6]

Charlotte says that there are those that are waiting until they are good enough. They have nothing particularly evil to point to that would hold them back from God, but they're waiting for some undefined state of perfection they want to reach before they feel they have a basis for standing in Christ's presence. She's saying, "Don't wait until this time comes." In the words of another hymn, "If you tarry 'til you're better, you will never come at all."[7] Just give yourself to God and let him do the perfecting. Then she wrote:

Just as I am and waiting not
To rid my soul of one dark blot.

She's saying there are some that can point to a specific habit or characteristic they haven't yet overcome and they are waiting to rid themselves of this one dark blot in their own strength before bothering Christ with it. But Charlotte says you ought not to wait. You'll rub at it forever and never clean

---

[5] Psalm 40:6-7
[6] United Methodist Hymnal 357
[7] United Methodist Hymnal 340, Stanza 3

it up yourself. Let God use his blotter on the blot. Then she sang,

> Just as I am, though tossed about
> With many a conflict, many a doubt.

Here she's saying that there are those that must know the ins and outs, examine all the doctrines, pick a particular church, have all their doubts resolved, all their inner conflicts removed before they feel at home in the presence of God. They recognize the inner struggle that confronts most Christians and use this as an excuse for non-participation in his Kingdom and his claim on their lives. She says don't wait until all your doubts and conflicts are resolved. The Christian life itself is a wrestling match where we wrestle not against flesh and blood, but against principalities, and powers, against the world rulers of this present darkness. Don't wait, but begin now to face your doubts and fears with the help of the armor of God. Come to him just as you are and he'll help you.

And so it is that the climax of assurance comes for the Christian—

> Just as I am, thou wilt receive,
> Wilt welcome, pardon, cleanse, relieve.
> Because thy promise I believe,
> O lamb of God, I come.

I heard Tony Campolo tell about being asked to be a counselor at a Junior High Camp and he said, "Everybody ought to be a counselor at a Junior High Camp, at least once."

He said, "You know I have some disagreements with the Roman Catholic Faith. I don't believe in the infallibility of the Pope and some other things." But after this experience he said, "I do agree with one doctrine of theirs—Purgatory. There is a place between heaven and hell where people suffer for their sins, and it is called Junior High Camp."

He was in charge of eight boys in his cabin and one of them had a touch of Cerebral Palsy and had difficulty walking and talking. Billy walked with a slouch and he talked with a halting, exasperating effort as though each word was going to be his last. And Tony said, "I was not prepared for how cruel Junior Highs can be."

On the first day there he saw Billy as he limped across the campus, but right behind him was a line of every boy in his cabin—mocking his every spastic motion as he limped, and giggling as they all limped along.

The next day he heard Billy ask for some directions from one of them. He said, "Which way to the craft shop?" It seemed like it took five minutes for him to get it out. And the boy answering him mocked his every halting effort. He said, "That way, Billy!"

But the climax of cruelty came when the boys had to choose somebody from their cabin to give the devotional to the whole assembly of 120 kids. And, you guessed it. They chose Billy. They could hardly wait to get him up before everybody so they could mock and snicker. Strangely enough Billy accepted immediately and on the last night he haltingly made his way up to the podium. Out in the audience they mocked him as he went. He got to the microphone and he began, "Jesus loves me—I love Jesus". It looked as if it would take him ten minutes to get it out. He went on, "Jesus loves you—and I love you!"

When he finished there was an awesome silence over the whole group. One boy from his cabin started crying and it unleashed a flood of tears in the whole camp. Revival broke out that night.

Years after that in his speaking and travels, Tony would run into some of the boys that were there in his cabin that summer. One would be a minister, one a missionary, another an outstanding layperson in a church. Invariably they'd say to Tony, "You remember me? I was at that Junior High Camp where you were the counselor. You remember that boy, Billy? I found God that night—or Jesus called me that night."

Tony said, "You know we had tried everything to reach those kids that week. We had a Philadelphia Philly to come in there and testify that since he had found Jesus he was hitting more home runs. It didn't faze them. We had a Philadelphia Eagle wide receiver that said since he'd found Jesus he was catching more passes. We even had Miss Philadelphia that came and said she had found the Lord and prayed and look what the Lord had done for her. None of it had any impact. But when Billy got up there I guess everybody on that campus really understood for the first time what Paul meant when he said, *"God chose what is foolish in the world to shame the wise; God chose what is weak in the world to shame the strong."*

You see, Billy came *"in weakness and in fear and trembling, (his) speech and (his) proclamation were not with plausible words of wisdom, but with a demonstration of the Spirit and of Power."*[8] It wasn't that it was a conscious calculation, but somehow every camper there looked up there at Billy and thought, "'If God can do this powerful thing through Billy with all his limitations, what might he do with me if I come to God JUST AS I AM?

Can we come to God just as we are?

---

[8] I Corinthians 2:4

NO KING BUT CAESAR?
Matthew 22:15-22, John 19:14-16

At the trial of Jesus the crowd cried, *"Crucify him!"* And Pilate said, "Shall I crucify your king?" Then the crowd said, *"We have no king, but Caesar!"* Those who crucified Christ said, *"We have no King but Caesar."*

Who was Caesar? In the day of Christ he was Tiberius. He was head of the empire. He was moody, jealous, suspicious, and ferocious. He represented national power. Loyalty to him was loyalty to Rome, and Rome was interested in power and wealth and what was good for the Roman Empire, nothing else. It was to all of this that you gave your loyalty when you said, "We have no King but Caesar." Is Christ still crucified by those who have no King but Caesar?

Could we be more guilty today on this count than those who crucified him? They were only fooling. They only claimed to be loyal to Caesar and claimed that Christ was an enemy of Caesar so that they could get Pilate to turn him over to be crucified. They still looked for their Messiah King to come. They thought Christ was an imposter. They knew Pilate would have to destroy anyone that set himself up in Caesar's place. They only claimed loyalty to Caesar as a trick to get Christ killed. But, what about us? Do we truly have no King but Caesar?

You take the way a blind loyalty to your nation and section has become more important than anything else to many people. We have some people who make "being a southerner" into a lifetime occupation. We have some people who believe that the only significant thing that God ever did was to make an American. He started off somewhere in darkest Africa and made the black people, then to the far East to make the yellow people, then the Northern Europeans, and

---

[1] John 19:14-16

finally he makes an American and he sits back and says, "It's good! It's enough. I can do no better. Amen."

We live in a land that has national power, a land promoting nationalism. We're not different in this; there are some 200 to 300 other nations set up under the same basic pattern that have nothing above, nothing beyond the state. They can claim the final allegiance and loyalty of all their citizens; they can conscript your children and send them out to die and take your money on the 15th of April. We live in a world of nationalism. A long time ago a politician, Stephen Decatur, said, "Our country, in her intercourse with foreign nations, may she always be in the right; but our country, right or wrong."

In one of his ads for congress, one candidate said he'd fight for you in congress if you were in the right. But he added, "If you're from my district, I'll fight for you if you're wrong." Right and wrong, God and conscience are to be twisted and bent in the direction of our national or even sectional loyalties.

You take the way we've put wealth and things above other values in our country. I read an editorial recently that said, "In this nation we are developing our appetites and starving our purposes." That's right. We're the only nation in the world where our biggest problems are getting fat, where to park your car and where to get enough air for humans to breathe after the cars get through breathing.

It may be a false prosperity we have. A rural philosopher said, "Folks buy so much on time, they ain't got no time left." But still it is prosperity. We're developing our appetites and starving our purposes. We take it as our right to have so much abundance. We can know what our missionaries tell us is true. We can see it on our television screens. You can walk the streets of countries where 15% of the people sleep on the street every night. You can see the little bellies of children protrude, not because of too much to eat, but because of malnutrition and hunger. They just protrude and explode. We have our own homeless and our own struggling social service institutions that can hardly scrape up enough income to stay in service to the poor. Yet we go on with our presumably, pre-emptive war to the tune of billions of dollars and assume that this is all right and the only thing we can do. Someone wrote, "A Salute to A Nine-inch Gun."[2] It went:

> Whether your shell hits the target or not,
> Your cost is five hundred dollars a shot.
> You thing of noise, and flame, and power
> We feed you a hundred barrels of flour.
> Each time you roar your flame is fed
> With twenty thousand loaves of bread.
> Be silent! A million hungry men
> Seek bread to feed their mouths again.

You know what this is like? It's like an irresponsible member of the family who spends all the grocery money on firecrackers. We're like the man who drinks beer and shoots pool all day when his little children need shoes.

It is astounding to see the self-interest of those who have no King but Caesar. Right is what is right and best for me, my family, my class, my church, and my nation. A ten-year-old boy asked his father for a definition of "ethics." The father said, "Well, son, I can't define the word *ethics,* but I'll give you an illustration. Your Uncle Henry and I are in business together. Now suppose a man comes into the store and buys a ten-dollar article. He gives me a twenty-dollar bill, thinking it is a ten-dollar bill and leaves the store. After he has gone, I discover the mistake. I say to myself, that man gave me ten dollars too much. That, my son, raises the question of' *ethics.* Do I put that extra ten dollars in my pocket or should I split it with your Uncle Henry?"

When Caesar is our only king and self-interest our only law, that's all there is to consider—just me... and maybe

---

[2] P.F. McCarthy, c.1915, published in *The New York World*

Uncle Henry. There is no higher throne to render a decision of right or wrong.

One of our Georgia political officials said, "Now is the time to settle every question that arises on the basis of what is in the best interest of Georgia." That's Georgia righteousness. We'll operate on the principle, GEORGIA FIRST. That would be like my saying at breakfast one morning when our children were growing up, "Now children, from henceforth we will operate on the principle, WATSONS FIRST. It's we first, then maybe Uncle Henry. Do we have no king but Caesar and help crucify Christ?

Contrast all this with the spirit of Jesus. Jesus had no King but God. His first public word was, *"Repent for the Kingdom of God is at hand."* The devil tempted him in the wilderness and said, *"Fall down and worship me. I'll give you the whole world."*

Jesus said, *"Get thee hence, Satan, for it is written: Thou shalt worship the Lord thy God and Him only shalt thou serve. No man can serve two masters. Either he will hate the one and love the other or he will hold to the one and despise the other. You cannot serve God and mammon."[3]* Jesus was a one-God man. He had no King but God. He said, *"Seek ye first the Kingdom of God,"* and all these television sets and gadgets and automobiles and national security will be added unto you. *"Seek ye first the Kingdom of God."[4]*

A little girl, who had learned percentages at school, was watching her father prepare his income tax. She noticed the column for his adjusted gross income in line 9 and she noticed the amount he gave to church and charity. She compared it to the amount he had to pay in taxes. She said, "Look, daddy, the government gets more than God does." That's right. Tobacco gets more than God does in America. Liquor gets more than God does in America. Drugs get more than God does in America. The lottery gets more than God does in Georgia. We

---

[3] Matthew 6:24
[4] Matthew 6:33

say we believe in God, but we give our money to the other gods.

Seek ye first the Kingdom of God...There's the Sunday worship service at church. But of course, there is the oversized Sunday newspaper with the cottage at the lake. You see, I only have one day to relax... I work so hard... I only get to be with the family just every other Sunday, just every long weekend.

Harry Denman said he heard Mrs. Arthur J. Moore pray this prayer and it helped convert him: "O Lord, if I love my husband, my children, my home, or anything more than thee, keep me from having them." She said it's when you love God more than anything else in life that you can truly love everything else in life. You love your family more when you put God first than when you don't.

Can we like Jesus come to the place where we have God as King? Our hope lies in the fact that nothing fits together; nothing comes out right with us, until we do have no King but God. The little boy buttoned his sweater and had one button left over at the top. So he re-buttoned it and had one left over at the bottom. Finally he buttoned it again and it came out right and he said, "Mother, I found out if you get it started right at the bottom, it comes out right at the top." If we seek first the Kingdom of God, everything will come out right.

But if we don't, everything will come out wrong. Until we seek God first in our world, the nations will just be like angry dogs barking behind iron fences. Until we seek God first in the church, it will just be a place that intensifies all the tensions and anxieties we feel in the rest of the world. Until we seek God first in our nation, it will be another kingdom that just comes toppling to the ground like every other kingdom that has made Caesar its King. Until we seek God first in our personal lives, we will experience that emptiness that makes drudgery of our days and nightmares of our nights.

This is our hope. *"Seek first the Kingdom of God"* is not just good advice. It's the hard grain of the universe. If we don't get this straight, we don't get anything else straight.

Is there room here for love of country? Of course! I agree with Bishop Arthur J. Moore who said, "I for one see no conflict between love of God and love of country." It is only as we love our own country, our own people, our own kinfolk, our own traditions and our own heritage... it is only as we truly love them that we can understand what the love of other people for their nations and their sections must be like. But God and conscience, right and wrong, truth and justice are never to be bent, never to be twisted in the direction of our national or sectional loyalties. This is making Caesar our God. True patriotism is concerned not only with material but spiritual welfare... moral and-ethical welfare. But when national power is king, when people cry, *"We have no King but Caesar,"* Christ is crucified by those who have no King but Caesar.

In fact, the scholars tell us that this is exactly what crucified Christ. It was the alliance between the state and religion—no separation between Church and State. It seems so impossible and petty in retrospect, but the high priest and the religious people persuaded the Roman authority that represented Caesar that Jesus was a threat to peace. Here was a man who said, *"My kingdom is not from this world. If my kingdom were from this world, my followers would be fighting to keep me from being handed over...* [5] Jesus had no conflict with the state. He was no threat to Rome or the religious establishment in Israel. He didn't want the state's tax money for his faith's purposes. When they asked him, *"Is it lawful to pay taxes to Caesar or not?"* He had even said, *"Give to Caesar the things that are Caesar's, and to God the things that are God's."* There's room for both church and state in separate realms. We might even say, "What Jesus

---

[5] John 18:36

has put asunder, let no one join together." But they wouldn't have it. They said, *"We have no king but Caesar!"*

I'm glad I wasn't there that day that they delivered him unto them to be crucified.

I'm glad I wasn't there when he bore the weight of that cross up that hill to Golgotha.

I'm glad I wasn't there to mock him, "King of the Jews!"

I'm glad I wasn't there to see them gamble for his robe.

I'm glad I wasn't there to put vinegar to his lips.

I'm glad I wasn't there to see his mother's eyes.

I'm glad I wasn't there to watch him die.

I'm glad I wasn't there... or was I? Could I have been there? Could I have been there because I, too, have no King but Caesar? Were you there?

> Were you there when they crucified my Lord?
> Were you there when they crucified my Lord?
> Oh, oh, oh, oh...
> Sometimes it causes me to tremble, tremble, tremble.
> Were you there when they crucified my Lord?[6]

---

[6] Afro-American spiritual

ON CHANGING OUR NAMES
Genesis 32:22-31, John 1:35-42

There's an almost universal affirmation of the importance of names in human life. Many of us want to escape childhood nicknames that seem to indicate less than mature, adult powers of decision and autonomy. Though I loved growing up in Baxley, Georgia, one of the consolations in leaving there was escaping the name "Hampy." I know of at least two maturing young people in my last large congregation—one from an affluent home, and one from a background of deprivation and poverty—who during my pastorate there consciously shifted the names they were originally called by their parents to the second name given them. I have a suspicion that it has something to do with their asserting for themselves a new, autonomous image of who they are and who they want to become as persons in their own right.

Names were no less important in the Bible. It contains 1,050 verses that incorporate the word "name' in them. I got out my concordance and counted them. This doesn't even include the times when people were addressed by their names, or given names by which they were to be called which signified something important about the character of the person. The people of the Bible believed that there was power in a name. The name of God was so awesome and powerful in their thought that they couldn't utter it. The name "YAHWEH" comes from their just using the consonant letters in the Hebrew to signify when they were even just breathing the idea of God. And when God is revealed to Moses in Exodus, God says the name of God is "I am who I am, or I will be who I will be". You can't pin me down or get a handle on me or control me. I am the active living God, the becoming God, who calls you to be whom I would have you to be.

And in our faith the names for our Lord Jesus Christ play such an important role. Just to say that says so much. "Lord"= one who rules us. "Jesus" = one who saves us. "Christ" = the anointed one, or the one anointed or chosen by God. "Messiah" is another way to say it.

So when John the Baptist sees Jesus walk by and says, *"Look, here is the Lamb of God!"* he wasn't just talking through his hat or passing the time of day. He was announcing a whole new perception of Jesus—not the expected military Messiah, but one who would conquer with vulnerable, suffering love. As the later John put it in Revelation's final vision, *"Between the throne and the living creatures, there was a lamb standing as though he had been slain."*[1]

In the New Testament, Jesus was always getting his name changed. In our passage, Andrew, Simon Peter's brother, moves from calling him just "Rabbi" which is a human teacher, in that day not even on the level of the ordained priest-hood, to calling him "Messiah." "We have found the Messiah!"

But I guess the important thing to us is whether our own names can be changed for the better. It must have been important to Jacob in the Genesis story. What a name to have! Jacob, the supplanter, or the heel-grabber. He got it from his birth when in the womb he grabbed the heel of his first-born twin, Esau, to try to get ahead of him into the world. So when the God-figure in this wrestling match by the Ford of the Jabbok asks him, "What is your name?" he has to say it, "Uh, Uh, Grabby." He had lived up to it. Remember the plaintive cry of Esau, *"Is he not rightly named Jacob? For he has supplanted me these two times. He took away my birthright, and look, now he has taken away my blessing."*[2]

But not content to remain "Jacob, Supplanter, Selfish Heelgrabber, Grabby", he strives with God and asks him to bless him. He says, "I will not let you go unless you bless me."

---

[1] Revelation 5:6
[2] Genesis 27:36

And God responds, "You shall no longer be called Jacob, 'Grabber,' but Israel 'Striver,' for you have striven with God and with humans and have prevailed."[3]

Note that the new name he has doesn't mean he has necessarily arrived. He's a striver with God. There's something here of our Methodist emphasis on "moving on to perfection." Not having achieved perfection, but moving on to it—striving toward the image that's been placed on us by God. A Cartoon showed a woman happily waving her diploma in the air, while someone standing alongside her is saying, "Now that you've got your BA, when will you go on to learn the rest of the alphabet?"

And in this same tradition, when Jesus did his name changing with Simon, he obviously didn't expect it to be an immediate, full-blown conversion. Andrew *"first found his brother, Simon, and said to him, 'We have found the Messiah.' He brought Simon to Jesus, who looked at him and said, 'You are Simon, son of John. You are to be called 'Cephas' (which is translated, Peter)."*[4] Jesus renames Simon, Cephus, or Peter, or the rock. When he did this he knew how far he was from being a rock. So why does Jesus declare this disciple, who will soon display all the fortitude of sand, or squishy mud at best, to be his "rock"? Why? Because it, too, is a name to strive after, a name to wrestle with and struggle against.

It's only after Jesus' crucifixion and resurrection that Peter begins to truly inhabit his new name. But the amazing grace of Christ always sees the possibilities in unpromising people and if we're open to it, he gives us a new name.

I guess all I'm talking about today is that we don't have to stay the way we are. We can change our names. Day's first cousin, Clebie, though a Methodist went to Bessie Tift Baptist College at Forsyth, Ga. back in the dark ages when Methodists and Baptists argued about such inconsequential things as to whether once you're saved you're always saved. It was eternal

---

[3] Genesis 32:28
[4] John 1:42

security for the Baptists as opposed to free will and falling from grace for the Methodists. Since Clebie had grown up in a good Methodist home where we not only believed in "falling from grace" but also regularly practiced it, she got into an argument with one of her Baptist professors about this doctrine. He said, "Miss Scott, you were born a Scott, you are now a Scott, and you will always be a Scott." Clebie rolled those Southern eyes and said "I shuwah do hope not!" And the class disintegrated. We can fall from grace, or we can find "Amazing Grace." We don't have to stay the way we are. We can change our names.

Of course none of us can do anything like this on our own. Dr. William B. McClain told about meeting a South Korean tailor in Itaewon, Seoul, Korea, named Smitty Lee. When Dr. McClain asked whether the name "Smitty" was Korean, the tailor told the story of his life being saved during the Korean War by an American soldier from Virginia who was called Smitty Ransom. The tailor further explained a rather familiar custom in that Asian culture and summed it up in two simple sentences: "He saved my life. I took his name." That's what happens when we really encounter Jesus. He saves our lives, and we take his name.[5]

I got word that my boyhood buddy, Billy, had died the first Tuesday of January. He was my childhood chum, best man at my wedding, but since then our paths parted and we'd only seen each other at most three or four times. My first memory of him was when they moved back to Baxley when he was five. He turned six thirty days after me as we started the first day of school together. Being brusque and bullyish, the first mistake he made that day was picking on Bobby Dubberly who was a little kid. But Billy had not yet learned the principle that "the littlest potatoes are the hardest to peel." So Bobby proceeded to thrash him. I couldn't let that happen

---

[5] Zan Holmes, *Encountering Jesus*, Nashville: Abingdon Press, 1992, 18-19

to my newfound friend so I plunged into the fray to help Billy. Having learned his lesson, Billy backed off, but Bobby continued and gave me a whipping I'll never forget for meddling where I had no business.

Billy the Bully and I continued our friendship as I would take my life in my hands to get in a car with him going the seventeen miles from Baxley to Hazlehurst in fifteen minutes during my teen years. I knew then that Billy would never lead your normal, sedate lifestyle. In the years that followed he went through two early marriages, incessant bouts with alcoholism, but founded a highly successful business that finally ended in bankruptcy. Never in church, though his Daddy had an end seat on a pew and his Mama sang in the choir all her life. So when word of his death came, I wondered how the family would take it. His dad had died. His Mama was ninety-four, so I called her and found she'd had a slight stroke and couldn't talk well on the phone. But his sister said she was taking it mighty well. You see, Billy, knowing he had a terminal illness, had shielded his mother until the very last. But his mother had been up Monday to see him and sat and held his hand as she watched him die. The sister said she now seemed broken hearted but serene, if you could be both at the same time.

But his sister had a question for me, the man of the cloth. She said, "Hamp, do you suppose Billy was saved?" When she said this, I was so glad that I had already contacted Billy's current wife. She told me how they had had thirteen years of a good, solid marriage. Billy had joined Alcoholics Anonymous where he went twice a week, religiously. She said he'd been the most sensitive, kind husband to her that she could ever have wanted. He'd gotten his life back together and through his consummate skill at selling, had helped the new owners of his old company get it back on its feet.

I was able to tell his sister that it was my conviction that AA with its Twelve Step Program of recovery was patterned after time-honored principles of our faith—things like:

"Our lives had become unmanageable and only a power greater than ourselves could restore us to sanity",

"Turning our lives over to God as we understood God",

"Admitting to God, to ourselves, and to another human being the exact nature of our wrongs",

"Making amends to people we had hurt", and

" Carrying this message to others."

I was able to say to his sister, I'm in sales, not in management in this faith business, and I don't place people into cubbyholes in the afterlife, but that I could trust Billy to a merciful God who had helped keep him sober for thirteen years.

In fact, I think I know what happened that first Tuesday in January. I don't know how, or where, and I can't spell out the furniture or the particulars of it, but I think there was an encounter that went something like this. "Jesus looked at him and said, 'You are Billy the Bully. No! You are to be called William the Conqueror—one who has striven with alcohol and self and God and has prevailed.'"

John in the Revelation has the Spirit saying to the church at Philadelphia, *"If you conquer....I will write on you the name of my God."*[6]

We used to sing an old gospel song. I don't remember all the words, but I remember just a part of the chorus. Maybe that's because it's the most important part. It went,

There's a new name written down in glory,
And it's mine! Oh yes, it's mine![7]

Is that new name ours today?

---

[6] Revelation 3:12

[7] From *A New Name in Glory,* Music & Lyrics by C. Austin Miles

ON WHAT WE HAVE WRITTEN
Matthew 27:24-26, John 19:17-22

After consenting to the death of Jesus, Pilate refuses to change the sign he had put on his cross. He says, *"What I have written, I have written."* What is this? Is this like Martin Luther standing before the Council at Worms—threatened with death if he didn't deny the writings he had written?

They asked him, "Will you recant?"

He said, "I cannot and I will not recant. Here I stand; God help me, I can do no other." And the reformation was launched.

Oh No! With Pilate, this isn't the courage of his convictions. It sounds more like the stubbornness of a weak man who salves his pride by scoring a petty point against his enemies when he has lost the chief issue with them already. He had handed him over to be crucified. But with this little bit of obstinacy he could fool himself into thinking that he was really a strong man. "What I have written, I have written." Pilate has corrupted what is really a wonderful phrase. It's just a petty, petulant phrase of Pilate, but said in sincerity, it could be one of the finest things a person could say. "What I have written I have written."

Besides being courage to stand by your convictions, it could be recognition of responsibility for your own faults and failures. There are plenty of persons who say all their lives, "What I have written, somebody else has written." That is, somebody else is to blame for all my faults and failures. I understand that they have invented a computer so human that it can blame its mistakes on another computer.

I have a great concern for alcoholics, for those with whom drinking had gotten out of control, those who need rehabilitation, and need the love and concern of a community that knows how to work with them. But I have discovered that it's hard to work with any alcoholic who blames the sorry condition on circumstances or relatives or past experiences or job or boss or mother or father. Frank Crawley said, "I had a friend who drank heavily and I asked him why. And he said, 'Why Frank, I'm married to the meanest woman you ever saw. You'd drink too if you were married to that woman.'"

Frank said to him, "Oh she's not as bad as all that. I've seen her at church and she seems to be a very nice person."

This friend said, "Well, if you don't believe me, pastor, just go home and eat with me tomorrow night and see."

Frank went. He came back from that meal and he said, "You know, he was right. She was the meanest woman I ever saw, with her subtle nagging, digging, complaining, and comparing him unfavorably with other men. She was the meanest woman I ever saw."

Drinking is often excused on this basis, but many alcoholics with whom I have worked either abuse their spouse or are woefully irresponsible; and you always wonder why the spouse has been as supportive as they have. Most who drink should place the blame clearly on themselves and say, "What I have written, I have written."

Oh I know it's hard to find fault with oneself. Seeing fault in yourself is almost as hard as seeing faults in your children—like the woman who said, "I could see my children's faults, if they had any." Dr. Keith Dittman addressing a pharmaceutical convention in Los Angeles said, "The medicine most needed today is a responsibility pill. We need a pill that puts people in touch with reality and accuracy in the assessment of their own role in life." It would be nice if you could give it in a pill. But probably people will never come to recognize that they are responsible for their own faults and failures until down before an altar somewhere they say, "What I have written, I have written."

What I have written, I have written." When it's said sincerely could also be admission that you can't erase the consequences of all your erring acts in life. What you have written you have written and it stands. We've had an emphasis on the forgiveness of God in our faith, and we've had such a good cure for the commission of evil acts that we've really not been too concerned about committing them. After all, there's nothing for which you can't receive forgiveness. But even though forgiveness for anything is possible, some things can't be erased. We can't erase the consequences of those things that we've done.

I used to tell a story to my children about a little boy who got up on the wrong side of the bed one morning. The very first thing he did to show his displeasure at the world was to take the toothpaste and squeeze it out all around the edge of the lavatory. Not content with that, he went on down the street on the way to school and saw Mrs. Brown's apple tree. He climbed over the fence, climbed the tree, and shook all the apples off the tree. Not content with that, he went on down the street and passed the barbershop. He saw a man in there lying down to get a shave with his face all covered with a cloth, while the barber had to go into the back of the shop for just a moment. So he ran in quickly, took the scissors and cut all the man's hair off and ran out of the barbershop.

Of course, by the time the little boy got home from school that afternoon, his mother had the message about what he'd done and she met him at the door. She said, "Johnny, I've heard about the terrible things you've done today, and if you don't go back and undo every bad thing that you've done today, I'm going to whip you within an inch of your life."

This scared him so much that he ran back into the bathroom and gathered up all the toothpaste and put it back in the tube. He left there and ran on down the street and climbed over the fence and grabbed the apples and put them back on the tree; and they began to grow. He left there and ran back down the street to the barbershop. There was the man still lying in the chair. He picked the hair up off the floor; put it back on the man's head; and it started to grow. Then he ran back home, smiled at his mother and said, "Mother, I have undone everything that I did wrong today." She said, "That's fine, Johnny. You're forgiven."

Then I would say to my children, "What's wrong with that story?"

My youngest said to me, "Daddy, you can't put toothpaste back in a tube." That's right. And you can't put apples back on a tree and expect them to grow. And I'm living testimony that you can't put hair back on a man's head. There are some things that we can't undo.

We excuse things as moods that we are in. But some things said in moods leave deep wounds that people never get over in close family circles. There are some things that we should never do. Not doing them is much better than getting forgiveness for them later. An ounce of prevention is worth a pound of cure. The schoolgirl told her teacher she was going to write an essay on pins. Teacher said, "What's your angle?"

She said, "Pins save thousands of lives each year."

The teacher said, "How come?" The girl said, "By not swallowing them." Some things in this life are better never swallowed in the first place.

At a Rotary Club, a man said that when he was a boy on a farm in the mid-west, he helped his father with the horses. One morning, he and his father were having trouble getting the horses hitched and bridled. His father said, "Get a rope. He's afraid of the bridle."

The boy said, "If you don't like the way I'm doing it, do it yourself." He knew he'd done wrong when he looked over at his Dad who looked crushed. He looked suddenly old and wounded by the remark. He knew he should have apologized and asked for forgiveness but he didn't. After a few months he left home and never returned. After some thirty years, he heard his father was very sick. Now he knew he had to hurry home and ask for forgiveness. But as he arrived he saw the hearse, and the mourners coming in and out of the house. That day he went out to the corral. It was lonely and deserted. The fence posts were falling or had already fallen, but he could still see his father with his bowed head. He said, "For the rest of my life, I could see my father in that one posture only."

Oh I know God forgives. But I have to ask myself. What in my life is still unchanged—still unforgiven? Of what might I have to ultimately say, "What I have written, I have written" and it stands?

But think with me about this petty phrase of Pilate in one more way. It could be admission that you can't avoid a decision about Christ. Pilate was just scoring a petty point against his enemies when he said these words, but they held a terrible truth for his life, too. What Pilate had written he had written and it stands for the centuries to read as his decision about Christ. He allowed Jesus to be killed unjustly and he can never erase that decision. We say it yet, "Suffered under Pontius Pilate, was crucified, dead and buried."

And that's the story that will be told of Pontius Pilate all down through the centuries until the end of time—"Suffered under Pontius Pilate." By refusing to make a decision, he made one. Oh he wasn't going to. He took his basin of water and put it out before the crowd. He took his hands and he washed them and he said, "I am innocent of this man's blood." Yet the sound of the water swishing in Pilate's washbowl echoes across the centuries. Above the sound of the organ and piano or the guitars and drums of the praise choir, above the sound of the preacher's voice, above the singing of the Hymns, can you hear the sound of the water swishing in Pilate's washbowl?

PRAYER

O God, we know too well that "What we have written, we have written." Help us in what we're writing now to set things right as we trust in the one who on the cross said, *"Father, forgive them for they know not what they do."* Amen.

A CONTRAST AT THE CROSS
Matthew 27: 27-54, Mark 15:37-39

If you ever seriously look at the cross of Jesus Christ and the one who died upon it, you will inevitably be faced with alternatives—doubt or faith. And if you face these alternatives, it's certain that you'll decide for one or the other. It's always been that way. As it's true today, it was true on the day Christ died.

The first wing of this contrast is doubt at the cross. We find this feeling represented vividly in the Scripture by one of the thieves that was crucified along with Christ. We don't know too much about him. He was a thief or a robber or a bandit. He may have been a revolutionary against Caesar's government who was being punished by Rome. One tradition gives him a name—Zoatham. Zoatham and Jesus are hanging there in the hot sun on their crosses. The rulers and some of the people and the soldiers pass by reviling him and wagging their heads, and they say, *"If you're the Son of God, come down from the cross!"* Zoatham catches up the taunt of the people and in bitter mood, fighting back at his fate with all the violence of his unbridled soul; he sneers, *"If you're the Christ, save yourself and us."*

This is doubt, isn't it? The rulers and priests certainly don't believe that Jesus is the Son of God, the Christ, the Messiah, and the one who was to redeem Israel and the world. They ask him to prove it by coming down from the cross, but in their hearts they know he won't do it. The thief asks him to prove he's the Christ by saving himself and the two thieves who are dying with him, but he doesn't believe he can do it. Their doubt is expressed in the way they phrase their requests. They start off—"If." "If you are the Son of God." Contained in this "If" is the firm belief that he is **not** the Son of God.

I checked through the Scripture thoroughly and there is only one other place where Jesus is talked to like this. It's in the story of his wilderness temptation by the Devil. The Devil says to him, *"If you are the Son of God, command this stone that it be made bread."*[1] The crowd and the thief and the Devil doubt Jesus. They say, "**If** you are the Son of God."

But what if the thief and the crowd and the Devil were right? What would be true if Jesus were **not** the Son of God? Well, for over two thousand years, those who have worshiped and followed him and imitated his life have been deluded, mistaken, fooled. Here's a great movement in history in which his disciples have endured persecutions and yet have prevailed as "His truth goes marching on" and "the saints go marching in." Those innumerable caravans that have moved and marched under the banner of Christ—mistaken? That's hard to believe.

Now it might be possible to believe this, for there have been mistaken movements of many. Consider those duped disciples of David Koresh out near Waco, Texas who were ready to die for their delusions, those duped disciples of Osama ben Laden who took thousands of innocents to their deaths with them. Millions have followed mistaken movements. Consider Communism and all the other "isms." Something is not true just because millions have believed it. But we could never believe that certain Christians we have known personally and individually were deluded.

You'd never convince a man whose name was "After." The missionary E. Stanley Jones told about him. He said this African changed his name to "After" immediately following his conversion. He reasoned that all things were new and different and important "after" he met Christ, so he was going to reflect that new reality in his name as well as in his thinking and living. The thief at the cross expressed his doubt of the Master—"**If** you are the Son of God." But this is one character at the cross with whom we can't agree. We've known too many people who were better than people could be unless Christ were in them. When the word "After" is a

---

[1] Luke 4:3

Christian's middle name, you don't have a ghost of a chance convincing them that they're deluded. You certainly have no chance of convincing the ones of us who have known them.

But there at the cross was one with a conclusion about the matter entirely different from the thief's. It's the Roman Centurion. He provides the contrast at the cross. It was the Centurion's job to determine when Christ was dead. At the outset he was a scoffer, too. He obviously allowed his soldiers to mock Christ. He thinks, "This man must be a criminal." But unlike the others, he used his eyes and his ears. He kept an open mind as he watched the events of the crucifixion. No doubt he was deeply impressed by:

> Jesus' courage,
> By his refusal of the opiate,
> By, "Father forgive them for they don't know what they're doing."
> By the dawning evidence of goodness and greatness,
> By his loud cry of victory as he died.

So he allowed the facts to shape a new judgment. Most people have minds like concrete—"All mixed up and permanently set." Trying to get a new fact or opinion in is like trying to get a breeze to blow through a billiard ball. But not this Centurion. Roman justice had miscarried. He doesn't say, "**If** you are the Son of God." He says, "*Truly this man **was** God's Son!*"

> The flowers breathe it,
> The stars chime it,
> The redeemed celebrate it
> The angels rise up on their thrones to announce it—[2]

Truly this man was God's Son!

But what follows if our alternative is faith instead of doubt? In January of 1959 I heard Dr. Albert Trulock who was then serving as Pastor of Wesley Monumental in Savannah tell this story. Horace Freeman, the father of

---

[2] From Talmadge of Brooklyn

surgeon Dr. Tom Freeman of Savannah, grew up in a rural area in Reconstruction Georgia. His was a poor but proud family following the Civil War. One of the embarrassments of his childhood was when the Methodist Steward came around for the Quarterage for their little country church. In those days they didn't have an annual budget and pledge campaigns to underwrite the budget in advance. Administrative Board Members called "Stewards" would each take a list. Before each Quarterly Conference they'd ride up to each farmstead on a horse or in a buggy pulled by a mule and collect the "Quarterage", that is, the church payments or pledges. Out of this the pastor would get his salary for three months, and the District superintendent, or Presiding Elder as he was called in those days, would get his salary and the Conference Apportionments.

Horace was standing there when the Steward approached his mother. He said, "Mrs. Freeman, do you have anything you can give towards the Quarterage?"

Embarrassed, she looked down into her worn apron and said, "Josh, I'm sorry. There's not a dime on this place. Here's a dozen eggs to give the preacher, but we don't even have enough eggs to share any with the Presiding Elder."

Horace was just coming into his early teens. He ran back behind the barn with tears streaming down his face. He knelt down there and the prayer came tumbling out with the tears. He said, "O God, I'll be the Quarterage. So help me God, I'll be your man!"

If you are the Son of God? No! Truly this man **is** God's Son!

If the Centurion could speak to us today he might say, "Yes, I saw him die. Who am I? I'm an ex-soldier of the Caesars, and am now a soldier of the cross.". What about us? Am I a soldier of the cross, A follower of the Lamb, And shall I fear to own his cause, Or blush to speak his name?[3]

---

[3] The Methodist Hymnal, 1939, #284

FROM PALMWAVER TO CROSSBEARER

John 12:12-13, Mark 15:15-25
A First Person Drama for Palm or Passion Sunday

L et's allow Simon the Cyrenian to speak to us from the perspectives of the 1st and 21st centuries.

My name is Simon. My home was in Cyrene, on the coast of North Africa. I have come back to your time to tell you about the most significant moment of my entire life. It happened a long time ago, but I'll never forget it, and I'll never tire of telling about it. But I'm about to get ahead of my story.

I was born and brought up in the City of Cyrene though my parents were Jews. They had come there from Israel long before I was born, but they never deserted the faith of the fathers. My parents were both devout Jews. Many of the Jews around us gave in to the pagan surroundings, but not so in our home. We knew who Abraham and Sarah and Miriam and Moses and Ruth and Naomi and Amos and Hosea, and Isaiah, and Jeremiah were. Our God, Jahweh, was very real to us. Why is it that so many people lose their religious ties when they move into a new community? Why do they forget God, and neglect the synagogue, and disobey the commandments?

As I grew up in our home I was always hearing about Jerusalem and the temple and the holy places of our faith. Since I was a little boy I had longed to go to Jerusalem someday during the highlight of the Jewish year, The Feast of the Passover. My family had always been too poor to make such an expensive trip. I was grown, had established a successful business, had a wife and two boys, Alexander and Rufus, before I saw my chance to go. I couldn't take the whole family, but the boys were now old enough to be left to care for their mother.

So I set sail for Jerusalem and the Passover. When I got there I found the city overflowing with pilgrims like me. All the lodging places in the city had been taken, so I found a place to stay about two miles out from Jerusalem. Jerusalem really was an exciting place this time of year. I wandered through the turbulent streets. I drank in the loveliness of the temple. I sang the songs of Zion with the crowds that gathered, and deep in my heart I knew what the Psalmists had been talking about, *"I was glad when they said unto me, Let us Go into the House of the Lord." "How lovely are thy dwellings, O Lord most high."*

On my second day there which was the beginning of Passover Week, I saw a great crowd moving out toward the edge of the city. A man in the crowd shouted, "Come with us to welcome the King of Israel!" I thought, "What nonsense is this?" But since everyone seemed headed that way, I went along with the crowd. They were grabbing up palm branches along the way, so I did too. I soon saw what we were to do with them. As a man in white approached riding a small colt, garments were strewn down in his way and we all began waving our palms and shouting, *"Hosannah, blessed be the King of Israel that comes in the name of the Lord! Hosannah! Hosannah!"*

This was exciting. I enjoyed it immensely, and though I didn't understand exactly what was happening, I waved my palm as fervently as the next person did. I never got very close to the man who was riding the colt and I soon lost sight of him in the excited crowd. But I learned later that he was a Galilean, Jesus of Nazareth, and that many thought that he was the one promised by the prophets to redeem Israel.

After that, the Passover Week went by very rapidly and before I realized it, we had come to the last day—the day that was to be the climax of the whole week. It was the day that the High Priest would go into the Holy of Holies in the temple to receive a message from God. It was the day to which we all looked forward.

I began my walk to Jerusalem that morning with a light and glad heart. It had been a wonderful week. I couldn't wait to get home and tell the family about it and make my plans to bring Alexander and Rufus here when they were old enough to understand and appreciate the trip. I was thinking along this line when just as I went to enter the gate of the city, I saw a crowd coming out toward me. In the midst of the procession was a band of Roman soldiers. In their bullying way they were pushing the crowd aside to make way for three condemned criminals stumbling along the road bent beneath the load of heavy Roman crossbeams. Knowing Roman soldiers, I quickly stepped aside to let the little procession pass by, but I was curious enough to stay close enough to see everything.

It was the first time that I had been so close to a Roman cross. Do you realize what these instruments of torture were like? These crosses were not like the little gold ones your women today wear around their necks or your athletes wear from their ears. They were not bright and shiny like the ones that gleam from church steeples. These condemned men were carrying crossbeams fourteen to fifteen feet long. It was all they could do to just drag them along. But they had it to do. It was part of Rome's punishment. Before they nailed him to it, each man had to carry his own cross to the place of execution. You couldn't help but feel pity for these men who were passing now, although I had no idea what their crime had been, or why they were being executed.

One of the three men dropped behind the others. I doubted that he would make it to the top of the hill, for he was already staggering under the crossbeam. There was something familiar about him. Why this was the same man who had come riding into the city in pomp and ceremony on a colt at the first of the week. I thought to myself, "What a way to come in and what a way to go out!" Just as this man got opposite me, he fell to the ground. He lay there in the dust a moment and struggled to get up, but it was obvious that he was too weak. He was a strong looking person with broad shoulders and muscular arms. But as he lay there on the road,

I knew why he had fallen. The stripes on his back told the story of the Roman "cat o' nine tails." His back had been whipped with a leather scourge in the lash of which pieces of iron and lead had been tied. In addition to this, a band of thorns had been thrust down on his forehead. He was weak from the loss of blood. No wonder he didn't have the strength to carry that cross.

The Roman captain came back to where the man had fallen. He swore at him and kicked him. But swear as he would the man simply couldn't get up alone. I hated the cruelty of the Romans and despised them for the way they treated those whom they conquered. Suddenly the Roman captain whirled and gave me cause to hate him more. As the one who was standing nearest where the man had fallen, his eyes fastened on me. "Here, you there! Get under this cross and help carry it!" I turned as if to go, acting as though I hadn't heard and muttering something about being on my way into the city. But I felt strong arms being laid on my shoulders. It was no doubt that he meant me. And when Rome issued an order they meant for it to be obeyed. Looking at the spear pointed at me, there was nothing else for me to do but to stoop there in the dirt, get under that cross, and help carry it.

How I hated having to do it. It wasn't the physical weight of it. I had always been strong, but the shame and humiliation of it was almost more than I could bear. You wouldn't really understand unless you had been a Jew. I understand that you have a custom of knocking on wood or touching wood for good luck which roots back to the time that supposed pieces of the cross of Christ were sold by illegitimate elements in the Roman Catholic Church as indulgences, or good luck charms. So today, you touch wood for good luck or protection. But let me tell you that no Jew in that crowd wanted to touch the wood of that cross, least of all me. Not only was I being compelled to carry a cross like a condemned criminal, but, touching that cross would make me ceremonially unclean to participate in the Passover. It would ruin my whole trip to Jerusalem if I couldn't go to the temple today.

I was angry with these Roman Soldiers. I had resentment in my heart against the man who had fallen with the cross, and I was angry with myself for stopping to watch. My day was ruined, my plans interrupted. And, why? It was the sheer chance of it all. That's what made my blood boil. Why me? I was only one of a hundred who was standing there by the roadside minding my own business.

But before I could think along these lines too far, the man whose cross I was helping to carry turned and looked at me. And I have tried to describe that look, that face, but I've always felt that no words I had were adequate. There wasn't a trace of hatred in that face, even after the cruel way he had been treated by his persecutors. And when he looked into my eyes I felt my soul laid bare before him. There was love and tenderness in his look and I knew that he was sorry that I had been forced to carry his cross. There was something about him that changed my heart. I no longer felt resentment against him. In fact I began to feel that it was a high honor that I could help this person to carry his cross because he had something that was completely different from anything that I had ever known.

We soon reached Golgotha. At the place of execution upright poles were driven in the ground. The condemned man was stripped, his hands were nailed to the crossbeam, his body was supported on the pole by a block, his legs were lashed out in an unnatural position, and his feet were fixed to the upright stake so that they were just off the ground. I give you my word that as we stood there watching him die, we knew that this was no ordinary man. Now some were still scoffing and mocking. I saw the very man who had asked me to go welcome this man as the King of Israel at the first of the week standing there. He yelled at him to come down from the cross if he was the Son of God, but most of us were shamed. The sun hid its face and the earth turned as black as midnight. We heard him utter with his last breath, *"Father, forgive them for they don't know what they are doing."* By then, we all felt like the Centurion, who cried out, *"Truly this man was the Son of God!"*

I made my journey back home, but I was a different man. My wife noticed it immediately. The boys sensed it. And the first night I was at home they asked me what had happened to me in Jerusalem. I told them the same story that I've told you.

You might wonder why I'm telling the story to you. It's because I think that you people in the church today are so much like me, and you can profit from a story about someone like yourselves.

You are like me in the Church today in that you, too, have many palm-wavers. You have church members who are just commuters with religion—gallery Christians, who just come to church once in a while on big days to wave their palms just to be waving them with the crowd. They contribute little if anything financially. They use Sundays for sport and recreation. They never read the Bible. They never pray. They speak of God only in profanity. They're a pagan lot, more or less, thoroughly sophisticated. They like a good time, but they have never discovered the secret of true happiness. You have people in the church who are like I was, just spectators, joining in the fun, giving lip service to the excitement of the moment, waving their palms. And I'm afraid that like those who first waved their palms to welcome the Lord of Life, you'll find many in that crowd who continue to mock and help crucify Christ.

You folks are also like me in that you have often found unexpected, distasteful experiences to yield a blessing in disguise. How I hated this humiliating interruption of bearing that cross for Christ, but today I mark that moment as the beginning of my Christian life. I can't tell you the blessing it's been to me. Because of it, I was known in the early Christian community as the man who had carried the cross of Christ.

Because of it, my boys, Alexander and Rufus, became active in the Church at Rome. Because of it, my wife became such an outstanding Christian after my death that the Apostle Paul affectionately called her his mother. He spoke of my boy and my wife in the same sentence in a letter to the church at Rome, "Salute Rufus, chosen in the Lord, and his mother and mine."[1]

I didn't know that the rough soldier was doing me the greatest honor that could ever possibly come my way, but when I got to Calvary, I knew it was worthwhile bearing the cross for Jesus. You may be going along through life with everything going your way when some misfortune, or sorrow, or suffering will fall upon you like a bolt from the blue. But before you grow bitter or resentful at life, I beg you to ask first, "Can this be a blessing in disguise?" With God's help can I take this experience, which may or may not have been sent by God, and use it for my enrichment and growth, and maybe even a blessing to others?

You folks are also like me in a way in that you, too, have witnessed the weakness of the body of Christ. When I helped Jesus to carry his cross, it was his body that was weak. It was his body that failed him; it wasn't his spirit. He still had his face set steadfastly toward the cross. He was determined to do what was necessary to bring humankind to its senses even to the point of death. His spirit was strong. It was simply that his body was weak and exhausted.

And isn't it the body of Christ that's still weak? St. Paul said, *"Now you are the body of Christ."* [2] And when he said it he was talking to the church. It's still the body of Christ that fails him and needs to be strengthened. If you want to help Christ, strengthen his church. You can't ever forget that the Church is the body of Christ. His Spirit dwells within it. Never do anything to destroy or weaken it, but everything to build it up and support it. Support the Church with your prayers, your

---

[1] Romans 16:13
[2] Romans 12:27

presence, your gifts and your service, and you'll strengthen the body of Christ.

But as much as you people are like me, there's one point at which we're different and will always be different. It's this. I was **compelled** to bear the cross of Christ. They made me carry his cross, and I found joy I had never dreamed possible. But you are different. No one will ever compel you to bear his cross. You'll have to choose it for yourself. And if you don't choose it, you'll miss the greatest joy in service possible in this life. Jesus knew that this would always be a matter of choice on the part of his followers. Didn't he say it? *"Whosoever will come after me, let him deny himself, and take up his cross, and follow me."*[3]

But I believe that you **will** take up the cross of Christ. I believe that you'll support his cause and Kingdom. I don't believe that you'll have to be made to do it. I believe that you'll choose it for yourself. You might wonder why I have such confidence in you, when I had to be compelled to carry the cross. I believe you'll choose to bear his cross because you know what I didn't know back then. If I had only known that he was to die for me, I would have run to take up his cross.

I wouldn't have waited until they had bound him with thongs that bit into his flesh. I wouldn't have waited until he was struck on the head with the rocks and stones. I wouldn't have waited until his back was whipped with the leather scourge. I wouldn't have waited to see that rough, heavy beam on his raw and quivering shoulders. I wouldn't have waited until he swayed and staggered and fell in the filth of the street.

If I had only known that he was to die for me, I would have run to take up his cross. You know. You know. You know. Won't you run to take up his cross?

---

[3] Mark 8:34

JESUS CHRIST IS LORD
Philippians 2:11, II Corinthians 4:5

J esus Christ is Lord. This is the title of this chapter. But I think that you will recognize immediately that it is more than this. It is the clarion cry of the Christian Church through all the ages. Years will turn into decades, decades into centuries, centuries into eternity, but Jesus Christ will still be Lord.

One tackling a topic of such scope and magnitude might be overwhelmed. The only reason that I can attempt it is that I can remember what John Wesley said about it. He said, "Jesus Christ is Lord means so much that all I can do is preach Him and pray that the Holy Spirit will give the full witness." It breathes from every paragraph in the New Testament, it sings in every hymn of the church, it shouts from every act of service in his name. Jesus Christ is Lord.

Paul says, *"We preach not ourselves, but Jesus Christ as Lord."* Now it is hard not to preach ourselves as Lord. It's like the man who went into the phone booth, shut the door and sang, "Hail, hail, the gang's all here." We all have within us a conflict, an ego, a little man that says, "I want to be God." It's been here since the serpent told Eve that she could be like God. So we fail to "own his sway and hear his call and test our lives by him."

We want what we want when we want it.

We go where we wish when we please.

We run our own show as we like it,

And we seldom get down on our knees.

But against this spirit of our day, a character in the Broadway play, *Advise and Consent*, speaks these lines: "Only God can be God and get away with it." We dare not preach ourselves, but Jesus Christ as Lord. Do we own his sway? Do we hear his call? Do we test our lives by him?

But we are not through with ourselves when we merely refuse to preach our-selves as Lord. If Jesus Christ is Lord, you and I bear a special relationship to him. Paul goes on to make this clear: *"We preach not ourselves, but Jesus Christ as Lord, with ourselves as servants."* Paul opens his Letter to the Romans with these words: *"Paul, a servant of Jesus Christ..."* The RSV translates it "slave" so we will know what he is talking about.

A servant-slave in those days looked to his master for everything. He was one who was not his own, one who was bought with a price. A servant-slave, whether he was a plowman or one who managed the whole household, was one who was completely obedient and responsible to his master or lord and was his servant forever.

You see the problem of being a Christian is the problem of allowing yourself to be taken command of by the Living Christ. Our Christian life begins when we say, "All the knowledge I have about myself today, I commit to all I know about God through my Lord Jesus Christ."

Before you think that this slavery and service to Christ is like grudgingly knuckling under to authority, or cringing like a cur before his master, or trembling before a demanding tyrant, let's hasten to ask, "What is his service like?"

If we enter it with real commitment, we find that serving The Lord Jesus Christ bestows the highest honor that there is in this life. Jesus says: *"If anyone serves me, the Father will honor him."* [1] This is more than the reward we are to expect at the end of life when we hear our Father say: *"Well done thou good and faithful servant."*

The real honor that we have as Christians who are servants consists of the fact that our commission to service is no less sacred, no less challenging than that of Christ himself. Paul said, *"He emptied himself, taking the form of a servant."* In John, Jesus said, *"As the Father hath sent me, even so send I you and you and you."* [2] The honor that God offers us is this: that he will condescend to use us, to lean upon us, to call for our poor help, to give us a real share in his own agony in the saving of

---

[1] John 12:26b
[2] John 20:21

the sinful world. Christ expects that that will not scare us away, but thrill us and win us and draw us irresistibly... such faith has he in you and me.

If he is using me, the chief wonder of my life is that he could, for I know myself. I know my weaknesses and my sinfulness. I know how full of hypocrisy I am at times. Yet Christ would use me?

There is a legend that Gabriel and Jesus were looking down over the parapets of heaven after he had ascended and Gabriel said to him, "Lord, how are you going to spread your gospel now? How are you going to save this world?"

Christ looked down and said, "I've left those eleven in charge."

Gabriel said, "But what if they fail, Lord?"

Jesus said, "Well then, I have no other plan."

This is the honor. As Augustine said, "Without God we cannot, but without us, God will not." This is at the same time our highest honor and our greatest challenge. Serving the Lord Jesus Christ bestows the highest honor that there is in this life.

Then serving The Lord Jesus Christ provides the most perfect freedom that there is. There is no freedom in simply following your own desires, doing what you want to do all the time. I saw a cartoon of one of these modern nursery schools where the children were allowed to do anything in the world they wanted to do, except just one rule. They couldn't hit the teacher. They could throw mud on the floors; they could break toys, splatter paint, and anything they wanted to do. After a few days of this activity, one of the little boys is looking up at the teacher, with a broken toy in his hand and he is saying to the teacher: "Do we have to do what we want to do again today?" So the first desire for limits and order was born.

George Matheson, in his hymn says: "Make me a captive, Lord, and then I shall be free." You see, the servant is one that having no freedom of his or her own, discovers perfect freedom. The only ones really free are those who are completely devoted to some commanding cause or some compelling person. We are bound to be slave to someone or something.

As Paul himself reminds us elsewhere: "*You belong to the power which you choose to obey, whether it is sin whose reward is death or God whose reward is righteousness.*"[3] But we belong to some power; we are slaves to someone or something. It's no accident that Paul, who spoke of himself as the servant-slave of the Lord Jesus Christ, is the one who could write with so much enthusiasm about the glorious liberty of the children of God.

If you are going to be free, you have to be a slave. A lady once heard Fritz Chrysler play his violin. He played with such freedom and such beauty that she said to him after the performance, "Oh, Mr. Chrysler, I'd give all I have to play like that."

He said, "Madam, I did." He had to be a slave to the discipline of learning to play the violin to experience the freedom of playing it.

If only people could discover this about our Lord before they beat out their lives in meaninglessness. They fear his service; they don't want to be tied down. They don't want to be circumscribed. But Christ wants to give us freedom.

Martin Luther in *Table Talk* said, "Birds lack faith, they fly away when you mean them no harm." I didn't discover fully what he meant until one summer morning I was going over to my study and a lovely brown thrasher had become trapped in the social hall of the Rincon Methodist Church. As I came in the door he became frightened and began to flutter and beat the panes of glass with his wings. The bird was terrified by my presence, trying to get out of the room. I could have left, but I wanted to release this bird and let it out. But you know how

---

[3] Romans 6:16

they do .He flew right up into the top of the building. Then finally, I thought I saw my chance to let him go free. As he got over against a window, I went over and grabbed the window quickly and pulled it down. As I pulled down the top half of the window, the fear-crazed bird fluttered right into the crack and as I pulled the window down, it broke its neck. He fluttered once or twice and fell to the floor. I carried him outside and I saw that his life was gone.

I thought to myself, "People are like that. They fly away from God in Christ when he means them no harm. He wants to give them freedom. He wants them to fly into the heavens of happiness in service for their Lord, but they lack faith."

Christ said, "*Everyone who commits sin is a slave to sin, but if the Son makes you free, you shall be free indeed.*"[4]

You see, serving the Lord Jesus Christ provides the most perfect freedom that there is.

And serving The Lord Jesus Christ bears fruit throughout eternity. You know the most frustrating thing about life is death, or the fact that all our worldly strivings and achievements come to the same end. All that pleases is for the moment. You can be a hero on the football field one Saturday and a zero the next. You can be a big man in town one week and a grave in the cemetery the next. Thomas Gray walked around the big, impressive graves in the churchyard at Stoke Poges and wrote:

"The boast of heraldry, the pomp of power,
And all that beauty, all that wealth ere gave;
Awaits alike the inevitable hour.
The paths of glory lead but to the grave."[5]

This is the continuing frustration of life outside of serving Christ. We live and we work and we labor;   and we

---

[4] John 8:34
[5] Thomas Gray, 1716-1771, *Elegy Written in a Country Churchyard.*

accomplish a lot of things, but we do it all for nothing in the end.

But it is not so for the servant of Jesus Christ the Lord. Our service in its impact is not limited in point of time by our own passing, but it lasts the length of his Lordship and how long will that be? *"And He shall reign forever and ever"*[6]

There are people in the New Testament whom we know little or nothing about except that they were servants of Christ. Paul says, *"Epaphras, who is one of yourselves, greets you."*[7] I don't know Epaphras. I never heard of him until I read his name in this passage. But even though I don't know anything about him, he still greets all of us by what he did in service for Christ. What he did in service for Christ will outlast the Caesars. It will never end until the reign of Jesus Christ has ended.

This is the glorious thing. At Jesus' feet we trade the temporal for the eternal, the limited for the timeless. Service for Christ may not amount to much in the eyes of the world, but its worth lies in what the centuries have to say over against the hours.

That part of our lives that is dedicated to service to Christ and our fellow humans is immortal and invisible. During World War II a wonderful boy out in California was committed to go into the Methodist ministry. But he came to draft age feeling that he ought not to shirk his military duty to his country. He was morally opposed to war and a pacifist in his ethical outlook, but he felt that he ought to at least go into the Medical Corps and serve in some way. So he enlisted in the service and became famous in the Medical Corps as one who would go to help anyone in trouble anywhere.

He had been a broken field runner in high school football and he would go out in the field where people were trapped and bring medical aid to them. Once out in Okinawa some

---

[6] Revelation 11:15
[7] Colossians 4:12

boys were stranded in a foxhole and one of them was critically wounded. They sent word for Harry to come and help them. He started making his way toward their foxhole, running like a broken field runner, dodging shells. Just as he got in sight of their foxhole, a bullet hit him. One of the boys stood up straight and said, "It will take more than a bullet like that to stop Harry."

You know that's right. It will take more than a bullet like that to stop Harry because that part of our lives that is dedicated in service to Christ and our fellow humans is immortal and invisible. You can't stop it.

Some years ago, a young doctor serving in the Pacific as a Navy Corpsman saw the terrible conditions of the people of Laos and he was determined that after the war he would come back and help them. He did better than this. This young, frail-looking scientist with a ready laugh on his lips and the fires of Christian idealism in his eyes was able to enlist others and he formed Medico, (Medical International Corporation Organization). Through voluntary contributions, they would seek to take care of people in areas where they have little or no medical care. His work was gathering momentum while he served with a small staff at Laos when he learned that he had cancer. He had to come back for a dangerous operation to the states. While here in a hospital in Chicago, he received a poem paraphrase from the children of a favorite Texas family, the Womacks of Ft. Worth, Texas.

There was a popular song about a Texas badman at that time called, "*Hang Down Your Head, Tom Dooley*."[8] It happened that this young doctor's name was also Tom Dooley. So when they discovered that he had cancer, they sent him this song:

> "Lift up your heart, Tom Dooley,
> Your work will never die.
> You taught us to love our neighbor

---

[8] Author unknown

Not just to pass him by.
We'll pray for you, Tom Dooley,
Your cure and your patients, too.
We'll save our dimes and dollars
For work that's left to do.
Lift up your head, Tom Dooley,
Lift up your head; don't cry.
Lift up your head, Tom Dooley,
Cause you ain't agoing to die."

He didn't die from that operation. This was September 1959. He made ready to go back to Laos and a friend said to him: "Tom, surely you're not going back now, you don't know how much time you have left, especially if you go back into those steaming jungles."

Tom said, "It's not how much time you have, but what you do with it that counts."

You see, Dr. Tom remembered all his life a line of a poem quoted by his father "I must fill each minute full of sixty seconds worth of distance run." He went back to Laos and had to come back for another operation. One day during the third week of January 1961, Dr. Tom Dooley breathed his last breath while the whole world mourned.

You say, well, those children were wrong. No, they weren't wrong. Somehow I feel that the last phrase of that poem those children wrote was true.

"Lift up your head, Tom Dooley,
Lift up your head; don't cry.
Lift up your head, Tom Dooley,
Cause you ain't agoing to die."

For that part of our lives which is dedicated in service to Christ and our fellow humans is immortal and invisible. You can't kill it. It will last as long as He reigns and He shall reign forever and ever.

In Peter's sermon at Pentecost he cried, "*Let all the house of Israel therefore know assuredly that God hath made him both Lord and Christ this Jesus whom you crucified.*"[9]

When the crowd heard it they were cut to the heart. They cried to Peter and the apostles: "*Brethren, what shall we do?*" Well, Jesus Christ is Lord! What will we do about it?

Might I suggest the answer in the words of an old spiritual that we sing?

"If you love him, why not serve him,
If you love him, why not serve him,
If you love him why not serve him,
Jesus Christ is Lord.[10]

---

[9] Acts 2:36
[10] Afro-American Spiritual, 418 United Methodist Hymnal

YOU LIGHT UP MY LIFE
Isaiah 58:6-8a,10; John 8:12-14a, 20;
Matthew 5:14-16; Ephesians 5:8-9, 14

According to John, one of the things Jesus said that got him into trouble with the authorities was this—He said, *"I am the Light of the World."* In the church today we're so familiar with the concept and the words that it seems peculiar to us that anybody would get upset over it. But if we think about it a minute we see what a bold, audacious statement it was to those Pharisees—A carpenter of Nazareth who spoke with the uncouth Galilean accent—supplanting Moses as the most pre-eminent in the faith and claiming to be the Light of the World? John, who's telling us the story, recognizes the disturbing, blasphemous claim it was, because at the end of Jesus full statement, he has to explain why no one just outright immediately arrested him for it. He says in verse 20, *"No one arrested him, because his hour had not yet come."*

This **was** a bold and audacious statement—"I am the light of the world." But have you ever thought about the fact that on another occasion in the Sermon on the Mount, Jesus has already made an even more astonishing, unbelievable statement? He said to his followers, *"You are the light of the world."* He says to us, "You are the light of the world." Oh, we can believe that He is the light with the perspective of the centuries. But you and I the light of the world? How can this be possible? I think we can only conceive its possibility if we get the biblical perspective on it. How is it possible that we are the light of the world?

It's possible if we recognize that ours is a reflected light. As the moon reflects the more glorious light of the sun to pierce the darkness of the night, so the followers of Christ are but a reflection of his glory. This is spelled out for us when Jesus says, "Let your light so shine before others, that they may see your good works and give glory to your father who is in heaven."

Now, there are some that go about the business of doing good works according to the Scripture, "He that tooteth not his own horn, verily the same shall not be tooted." But when true disciples do good works, they don't presume to be the true original light themselves, nor do they try to call any attention to themselves. The Scripture says of John the Baptist, "*He was not the light, but came to bear witness to the light.*"[1] So when we today do good works to let our light shine, it's not the meritorious deeds of the disciples that call attention to themselves, for the world which sees them doesn't praise the disciples for them, but the heavenly father.

The valiant little Episcopal Church in Bainbridge hosted a feeding program five days a week for the elderly poor. They did it so effectively for several years that when they finally had to give it up, the city itself saw the value and necessity of taking over the hosting task. Before we knew that the city was going to take it over, I wondered if **our** church ought to do it, and I wondered, "How many letters of thanks from the community has the Episcopal Church received for providing this site for so long?" Upon reflection I think it was the wrong question. The good works of a church aren't designed to draw attention to **it**, but as reflected light to bring glory to the Lord of the Church who feeds the hungry with good things.

But the world is grateful for even reflected light. They had a storm up at Emory in Atlanta on the last night of Minister's Week, and as I was making my way back, I was stopped by a tree across Lullwater Road late at night. The storm had thrown all that side of Atlanta into pitch-blackness. And as I turned my car around to make my way through Atlanta on less known roads, how grateful I was for the light of the headlights on my car that showed the way. Those headlights weren't the sun, or even the moon that was clouded out. They weren't the powerful mercuries of the streetlights, but these lesser lights were enough to see me home through the pitch-black eeriness

---

[1] John 1:8

that prevailed from Emory halfway to Griffin. How is it possible that we are the light of the world? It's possible if we recognize that ours is a reflected light, but still desperately needed to pierce the darkness of the night.

It's also possible to believe that we are the light of the world if we're willing to pay the price of compassion. Dr. David A. McClendon, a great Presbyterian minister, spent the night in the home of Halford Luccock, that peerless teacher of Preachers at Yale Divinity School, shortly after Christmas. Dr. Luccock said, "David, I've just learned one of life's most important lessons. We were delighted when my son, Robert, decided to bring our eight and ten year old granddaughters home for Christmas. Before they came, I asked Robert what they wanted for Christmas so I could get it and have it wrapped up under the tree for them. He said, 'They want the world.'

He quickly explained that they wanted a globe. I thought that was a great gift to keep them from becoming parochial. I wanted my granddaughters to feel that they were citizens of the world." So, being the Scotchman that he was, he went to twenty-six stores all over town to find the finest globe at the cheapest price. He stored it in the attic until Christmas Eve when he came down the stairs with the world in his hands to wrap it and place it under the tree. When they all rushed in on Christmas morning, Dr. Luccock presided over the opening of the gifts with all the dignity of Vatican II, saving the globe until last. Then he handed it to the girls, saying "This is to you two girls from your Grandfather."

They opened it with anticipation that quickly turned to disappointment—said politely, "Thank you, Grandfather", found other toys and went off to play.

Dr. Luccock said, "Robert, what's wrong? You told me they wanted a globe."

Robert didn't know. He got one of the girls off in a corner and said, "Now, tell me the truth. I got the wrong thing, didn't

I?" She said, "Grandfather, you got us a dark world, and we wanted a lighted world."

You can bet, the next morning Grandpa waded through the trade-in crowds at the store, got another globe, wrapped it, brought it home, and watched with glee as his granddaughters opened it and with joy plugged it in. Together they watched the lights come on all over the world. The tight, Scotch Dr. Luccock said, "David, I learned my greatest lesson in this thing. I learned that a lighted world costs more."

Jesus knew that. He said, "I am the light of the world." But he knew what it would take to light it. For the cross loomed out ahead of him and in a day or two he would be saying, *"and I, if I am lifted up will draw all people unto me."* And when he told us, "You are the light of the world", he knew we couldn't be unless we, too, were willing to pay the price of compassion. It's not that he was trying to get us to go through some kind of self-sacrificing religious act like people in his day—fasting, going without food to show their religiosity, or like people today sometimes trying to give up a few pleasures for Lent. I heard about a guy who said he was doing this. He said, "I usually take my whiskey with water, but during Lent, I'm going to leave off the water and take my whiskey straight." Jesus knew God wasn't interested in such play-acting.

A long time ago the prophet Isaiah saw the connection between real acts of compassion and the ability to give off light. He has God saying to his people,

> *"Is not this the fast that I choose:*
> *to loose the bonds of wickedness,*
> *to undo the thongs of the yoke,*
> *to let the oppressed go free, and to break every yoke.*
> *Is it not to share your bread with the hungry,*
> *and bring the homeless poor into your house;*
> *when you see the naked to cover him,*
> *and not to hide yourself from your own flesh?*
> *Then shall your light break forth like the dawn.*

If you pour yourself out for the hungry
and satisfy the desire of the afflicted,
then shall your light rise in the darkness
and your gloom be as the noonday."

Socially concerned, compassionate acts precede the shedding of light. Sammy Clark who served as a missionary down in Peru was there during a terrible earthquake and flood. The Methodist Church had made very little evangelistic impact, but it came through in a shining hour. For before the Peruvian government or the World Health Organization of the United Nations, or the U. S. Government, or any other agency had gotten through their red tape, the United Methodist Committee on Relief was there with food and help for rebuilding. It brought a different attitude to the church overnight, for *"If you pour yourself out for the hungry, and satisfy the desire of the afflicted, then shall your light rise in the darkness and your gloom be as the noonday."*

I think any Evangelism that isn't accompanied by compassionate social concern in advance of it and as a part of it is empty froth. It's darkness rather than light. We'll never get to where we are standing on the promises while we're just sitting on the premises.

Oh a lighted world costs more. It costs more in sacrificial devotion, for if it's necessary, the wick must burn out for Christ. It's not an advertising light like a theatre marquee calling attention to itself, but it's like an altar flame continually giving itself up, or like the light of a lighthouse with its costly kilowatt-hours that points the lost sailor to the shore.

You can get a city or countryside without any church in it, without any culture in it, without any love in it pretty easily. You can forget prayer, Sunday School, Sunday Worship and all the special offerings for orphans, elderly, special needs children and adults, the hungry and the homeless. You can let others visit the shut-ins, carry food to the grieving and the poor and go on the work teams to restore devastated communities, but you'll never have a lighted community or a lighted world that way; because a lighted world costs more. The only way that we could ever possibly believe that we could be the light of the world is if we're willing to pay the price of compassion.

One other thing makes it possible to believe this audacious, bold claim for his followers that Christ made when he said, "You are the Light of the world." It's this. We know in our own experience that any light we have came from following a reflected light in others to its source.

Ask yourself why you're in church this morning and if you gave just a surface answer you might say, "Well, it's a habit!" or "It runs in my family." But if you were to seriously address the question of why you try to follow Christ, or attend Church, or do any worthy work in the church or community; you could probably point to some person in your recent or distant past in whose reflected light you saw the light of Christ.

Day doesn't like for me to tell this, but when I was pastor at Bainbridge, one Sunday, Barney Shepard sat down between his wife, Brownie, and my wife, Day, in the Slappey Sunday School Class. When Day smiled at him, he said, "Day, you light up my life!" He had to quickly explain that he'd been listening to Debbie Boone's hit record while working on cars at his shop. So when she smiled, it was on the tip of his tongue. I told Barney that that didn't surprise me, for long before that song was ever written, for over twenty-five years I'd been singing to her in one way or another—"You light up my life! You give me hope to carry on."

Maybe you saw it on television when Max Cleland, triple amputee from the Viet Nam conflict, accepted his post as Director of the Veteran's Administration from his fellow Georgian, Jimmy Carter. One of the things he said was this— "I asked God for all things that I might enjoy life, but God gave me life that I might enjoy all things." Just looking at that man gives others hope to carry on.

Jesus said, *"I am the light of the world."* But more than that he said, *"You are the light of the world."* Impossible? Not if we recognize that ours is a reflected light. Impossible? Not if we're willing to pay the price of compassion. Impossible? Not if we remember that any light we have came from following a reflected light in others to its source.

So maybe we ought to believe Jesus when he says, "You are the light of the world." Maybe we ought to listen to Paul when he says, *"Awake, O sleeper and arise from the dead, and Christ shall give you light."* Who knows? Maybe somebody will say it to us someday—"You light up my life."

MAKING THE MOST OF THE TIME
Ephesians 5:15-20, Galatians 6:10

One of the chief characteristics of our day and age is haste. We'll soon be able to go clear around the world in three hours. That's one hour for flying time, and the other two to get out to the airport.

People are in a hurry. I thought I was in a hurry at 6:25 A.M. I was headed for my tennis doubles at 6:30 and knew it would take me another 10 minutes to get there. I was going to be late. So I was going 35 mph on a 25 mph street. But I pulled up to a stop sign and the guy behind me who had been pushing his headlights into my bumper took this opportunity to run the stop sign as he roared around me. People are in such a rush to get there that many times they ignore the detour signs, just go around them and travel on down the torn up highway in the hope that they'll be able to get through. When one man did this one time, he found another sign on the back of the detour sign after he had been forced to turn around and come back. The sign read, "Welcome Back, Stupid."

But the fact that we're in a hurry is not the thing that worries me the most. The thing that gives me concern is that we're rushing on to get somewhere so fast that we ride right by our opportunities. People are so feverishly looking for some other place and some other time in which to make their lives count that they fail to make them count right here and now. I think that this is the root of all our haste. We have so little faith in our ability to do something and be something significant right where we live in the moment we live. So we rush vainly on looking for the time and place that we **can** do something important. We miss life now where we live because of our mad haste to find life somewhere else at some later time. I think that our hurry and haste are just symptoms of this deeper, underlying sickness.

Men thundering through the firmament,

On saving seconds grimly bent,
Have never time to pause and stare
At white birds arching down blue air.
And, hurtling headlong over earth
To earn an extra moment s mirth,
Have never time to understand
Long rhythms of the rolling land.
Have never time enough to gaze
At hills serene in smoky haze,
Nor ever time to stop and see
Green wisdom in a blowing tree.
They squander suns to save a day,
In hoarding nights fling stars away,
And in their hot pursuit of haste,
Let earth and heaven run to waste. [1]

If there are some of you who have never had the glorious opportunity of riding over unfamiliar country roads with me, you ought to speak to my wife, Day. I'm sure she'll be gracious enough to let you have her place in the car. The usual pattern is for me to study out very carefully where I'm going on the map and what turn I'm going to take, and then to ride so madly toward the turn that I ride right on past without taking it. Then I have to back up to get on the right road. This is what we do over and over and over again in our lives. We rush on to get somewhere so fast that we ride right by our opportunities.

Multitudes of people are dis-satisfied with the place in which they live. They think that nothing really significant could happen in the place they live. So they pass up any opportunities to be of good that they might have there. A very young man went as a teacher to a country school in Appling County. The school where he taught was out in the fourth district of the county, the most backward section. Nobody from out there had ever amounted to anything. It was a rough

---

[1] Poems of Jane Merchant

section where ignorance and drunkenness reigned. But just as if he didn't recognize the place as a hole, the man who later became Dr. Woodward, President of Emory College at Oxford, began to pour out his life in that little community.

He found a boy who had some sense but who could only attend school four months out of the year. He had to work for his father the rest of the time. Dr. Woodward helped the boy personally, bought him books, and enabled him to get his high school diploma over the opposition of his father. Dr. Woodward had to go on to a different place of service, but when that boy turned 21, he left his home and headed for college and worked his way through. He became a lawyer in Baxley Georgia, a senator in the state government, a teacher of the men's bible class of the Baxley Methodist Church for 20 years, and my father. I'll always be glad that Dr. Comer Woodward didn't feel that he was living in a hole when he went to the Fourth District of Appling County. He didn't pass up any opportunities to be of good because of the place he lived.

Multitudes of people are dis-satisfied with the time in which they live. They think that nothing really significant could happen in the moment they live in; all the really important things in their life are out in the future, and so they pass up any opportunities they might have to be of good right now. I know a girl now who used to be like this. At her five-year-old birthday party she leaned over and blew out the candles. She heard the raucous voices of the pigtailed girls and the spotless boys sing happy birthday and she ate a big piece of the delicious white cake. But she wasn't happy. She wasn't happy because she wished that she were six. And all through her life it was like that. She was always waiting to really live tomorrow, not today.

When she was five in kindergarten, if she could just start to school that would be real living! When she got in Grammar school, if she could just get into high school, that would be real living! When she got in High School if she just could graduate, that would be the day! When she was in college, if she could just get married, that would be real living! When she got married, if she could just have a child. That would be real living! When she got the child, if that child would just grow up, be more mature and quit acting so childish, that would be real living! That girl has changed now, and she lives in the moments as they come to her. She rejoices in the opportunities that come her way right now. But how many millions have not changed from this! How many millions are always waiting to really live tomorrow... not today? How many millions are always looking to the future for the meaning of their life? **If** I could just get a higher paying job, then what I would do. **If** I could just be a success in business, then what I would do. **If** this situation would pass away, then what I would do, but then, not now.

The tragedy of other place living and other time living is the tragedy of wasted opportunity. A man was sitting in the bus station in Macon, Georgia, waiting for a bus to Atlanta, and the time got heavy on his hands. To amuse himself he went over to one of these scales that not only tells you your weight but your fortune as well. He put in his penny and a little card came out. He picked it up to read it. It said, "Your name is Ronald Robertson. You are thirty-six years old. You have a wife and two children; you earn $45,000/year and you are waiting for a bus to Atlanta, Georgia."

The man was simply amazed. The information was exactly right. It was so perfect he thought there might be some trick to it. So he decided he'd put in another penny, and then if somebody who knew him had loaded the machine, he'd catch them by doing it again. He put the penny in and the card came out. It said, "Your name is Ronald Robertson; you are thirty-six years old. You have a wife and two children, you earn $45,000/year and you are waiting for a bus to Atlanta, Georgia." He reeled back in amazement. He couldn't get over it. He walked around in the bus station mulling it over. It couldn't be and yet it was. He decided he'd try it one more time. He walked over, he put in his penny; the card came out. It said, "Your name is Ronald Robertson. You are thirty-six years old; you have a wife and two children, you earn $45,000/year and while you've been fooling around, you've missed your bus to Atlanta, Georgia!" Do we miss our bus to life at its best when we fool around with other-place living and other-time-living? Could opportunities here and now be lost never to come again? Could we find ourselves to be victims of the tragedy of wasted opportunity?

How many times have you longed for the land of beginning again, where you might go back and do over a portion of your life? David must have longed for it: He said, *"O Absolom, my son, my son! Would I had died instead of you! O Absolom, my son, my son!²"*

Perhaps if one day back then in the then that was once the "here and now", David had lived more for his son, there wouldn't have been the necessity to die for him. But parents can die a thousand deaths because they were too busy to take their opportunities to do good when they came.

Opportunities to be kind knock on the door of our hearts and go weeping away because we are too busy. We're so eager to get to some other place and some other time when we will do something; and the something at hand goes undone.

"Four things come not back:
The spoken word, the sped arrow,
Time past, the neglected opportunity."³

Just before he left Emory to take a job in another school, Dr. Henry Johnson gave to us young theologians his prescription for living. One of the ingredients in that prescription was, "Take opportunities to be of use when they come. Don't rush on to your supposed destiny or cause and neglect real opportunities to be of service near at hand."

---

² II Samuel 18:33
³ Omar Idn Al-Halif

I found out later that Dr. Johnson was not the first person that said it. Paul said it to the Galatians, *"So then as we have opportunity, let us do good unto all."*

That text came alive in my own life only after I got out into a pastorate. When I took my first five-point circuit as a young preacher, I was consumed with a passion to get a job done. I had to get my preaching done; I had to get my administrative work done as a pastor; and I had to get my visiting done. I had set myself up a little schedule. I would study every morning; I would visit every afternoon; and I would preach every Sunday. I even outlined the places I would visit on each day of the week. I set up a goal to see every member twice a year. That was a pretty high goal with five churches scattered over the whole county with dirt roads. That was about all I could have done if I visited every day without any interruptions. But I found as I got into the work, that my little schedule was getting upset. It would frustrate me terribly. Meetings of preachers in the morning would break in; and revivals and bible schools and funerals, and weddings, and people in the hospitals in three different directions.

Because of all these things cutting in on my visiting time, I found myself speeding up my calls in the homes. I had to get in one house and get out of it in order to make my rounds. I began to view any call upon my time and energy like a personal problem in a family, or sickness involving a hospital call, as a frustrating interruption. It began to cast a pall down over my entire life until I began to see what I was doing. I was doing what Johnson had specifically advised us **not** to do. I was rushing on to my supposed cause and failing to take the opportunities to be of use near at hand.

O there's need to plan ahead, but could it be that our primary duty is not to see what lies dimly at a distance, but to do what lies clearly at hand? Stephen Grellet said, "I expect to pass through this world but once. Any good thing, therefore, that I can do, or any kindness that I can show to any fellow human being, let me do it now. Let me not defer nor neglect it. For I shall not pass this way again."[4]

Ephesians advises, *"Be careful then how you live, not as unwise people but as wise, **making the most of the time**, because the days are evil."* After the plot one week that the Brits foiled in which thousands were targeted for death in airplanes headed for the most hated nation in the world, we might conclude that our *"days are evil."* How then should we live in such days?

Edwin Markham tells how the Great Guest came to see old Conrad the Cobbler. Two of his neighbors drop by the old cobbler's shop and he tells them about the dream he had at dawn. The Lord had appeared to him and told him that he was coming to be his guest that very day. So Conrad pretties up the old shop with fir and holly, and gets out the milk and honey and bread for his very special guest. The day wears on. Conrad dreams about how wonderful it will be to have Christ with him.

> He would wash the feet where the spikes
> had been.
> He would kiss the hands where the nails
> went in,
> And then at the last would sit with Him
> And break the bread as the day grew dim.

Look as he might though, the Lord failed to appear. A beggar came by with bruised feet; and Conrad called him in from the stony street to give him some shoes. A hungry, lonely old crone, broken with sorrow with a burden of wood on her back came, too. Conrad straightened her load, gave her his loaf of bread with honey and sent her on her way refreshed. A little, lost child also came to his door. He gave it milk to drink and then "led it home to its mother's arms."

> The day went down in the crimson west,
> And with it the hope of the blessed Guest.

---

[4] Stephen Grellet, 1773-1855, French-born Quaker Minister

And Conrad sighed as the world turned gray,
"Why is it, Lord, that your feet delay?
Did you forget that this was the day?"
Then soft in the silence, a voice he heard,
"Lift up your heart; for I kept my word.
Three times I came to your friendly door;
Three times my shadow was on your floor.
I was the beggar with bruised feet;
I was the woman you gave to eat;
I was the child on the homeless street."[5]

"So then, as we have opportunity, (where we live, right now) *let us do good unto all..."*

---

[5] *The Best Loved Poems of the American People,* p. 297

ABOUT WEARING WHITE ROBES
Psalm 23, Revelation 7:9-17, John 10:22-30

In John's grand vision of the final end of all history, he has those in white robes gathered around the throne and the Lamb singing praises to God. These are obviously the "good guys," not just in white hats, but white robes, signifying they're the people completely covered in purity. These are the ones finally and forever approved by God.

At the heart of the passage, an elder rings out the question to John. He says, *"Who are these clothed in white robes, and whence have they come?"*[1]

John says to him, *"You know."*

And then the elder proceeds to give the answer that he knew all along. And he begins to spell out the qualifications for wearing one of these white robes. Now, even before the elder starts giving the qualifications, we know from the start of the passage and our whole biblical faith some answers that are wrong.

Who are these clothed in white robes? We know immediately that it's not the Ku Klux Klan or any of their cousins. People who can't get along with other races, or nationalities, or socioeconomic classes will be very uncomfortable in that crowd, because John has already said that they're, *"a great multitude which no man could number, from every nation, from all tribes and peoples and tongues."*

The first part of the 7th chapter with its reference to 144,000 is often used by so-called Christian groups to maintain that there will be a very limited number in heaven, and to assert, of course, that they're part of that very limited number and you and I are not. It's like the bumper sticker I saw on a cute little car in front of Day's hairdresser's shop a while back. It said, "Jesus loves you—but **I'm** his favorite! " But such a spirit can't be found in the whole passage.

---

[1] Revelation 7:19

Eligibility is wide open. We have here a picture of the vast assembly of the redeemed. If John had had access to the metric system and had known figures as large as the national debt, he would have used these instead of the 144,000 to indicate how large the assembly was. He's just following the Genesis tradition of 15:5 and 32:12 where it's anticipated that through Abraham and his seed "*all the families of the earth will bless themselves.*" And they'll be as numberless as the stars in the heavens and the sands of the seashores.

Our national rivalries and hatreds are shattered before such a vision. A member of my church at Park Avenue, Valdosta, told me about being coerced to go to church by his mother-in-law after he married a German girl following World War II. His mother-in-law taught the protestant faith in the German schools during the war in Hitler's Germany, and her daughter constantly worried that the Gestapo would haul her off to a concentration camp for the things that she taught in school. She knew Hitler was wrong about Aryan white supremacy and at times her faith caused her to have to express it in coded ways to her students. This member is eternally grateful that the spirit of revenge and hatred did not prevail in this nation that won the war. Instead of indiscriminate destruction of the vanquished, we inaugurated the Marshall plan to reconstruct a shattered Europe, including the residue of Hitler's Germany. For my member knows that that German lady will be wearing a robe up there and waiting on him if he ever makes it. This in spite of all the hate words of the conflict like "Bloody Huns and Crazy Krauts."

For, believe it or not, around the throne and the Lamb dressed in white robes there might be American and English, German and Japanese, French and Spaniard, Libyan and Russian, Croatian and Cuban, immigrant and native-born. And whether we get to robe up may be dependent on whether we can be comfortable in that crowd.

Who are these clothed in white robes? We already know before the elder speaks that it's not necessarily those who make the right noises. It's not necessarily those who claim to be "Born Again" or Baptized with the Holy Spirit", or any of the other popular, stereotyped expressions of Christian testimony.

In Miami, a while back, two robbery suspects killed two FBI agents and wounded five others before they themselves were killed. These two had no criminal records and were described as hardworking family men. Matix and Platt were linked to at least a half dozen bank and armored car robberies in Dade County during that year. Matix was called a "born-again Christian" who liked to give testimony in church to the memory of his dead wife. Do we need to be reminded, *"Not everyone that saith unto me, 'Lord, Lord', but he that doeth the will of my Father which is in heaven."*[2]

Who are these clothed in white robes? We know immediately that it's not those who have worked their way up to it by becoming worthy. The elder speaks, *"These are they that have washed their robes and made them white in the blood of the lamb."* [3] That's a gory thought! How can you get robes white by washing them in red blood? The point is that it's the life and death of Christ for us, not anything in ourselves that makes us worthy.

A parable: A man once went to heaven and was met at the gate by St. Peter, who said to him, "It will take a thousand points for you to be admitted. The way you have lived your life will determine your points."

The man said, "Unless I was sick, I attended worship every Sunday and sang in the choir."

Peter said, "That'll be fifty points. What else?"

Man said, "I always tithed my income."

Peter said, "That'll be twenty-five more points.

The man, realizing that he had only seventy-five points, began to get desperate. He said, "I taught a Sunday School Class for several years."

---

[2] Matthew 7:21
[3] Revelation 7:14b

Peter said, "That's great work for God, but it's only worth twenty-five points."

The man was becoming frantic. He said, "You know at this rate, the only way I can get to heaven is by the grace of God!"

Peter smiled and said, "That's worth nine hundred points. Come on in!"

It's not cheap grace, because he died for us. But the only way to get a robe is *"by grace, through faith."*[4] The very life poured out on the cross enters the lives of people to make them something different from what they were, and it's not our own doing, it's the gift of God!

Who are these clothed in white robes? The elder begins to outline some positive things. They're *"before the throne of God, and serve him day and night within his temple."*[5] It must be folks who enjoy worship here if that's what they're going to do for eternity. I know the little boy said to his grandmother, "Grandma, if you ever went to one circus, you'd never want to go to prayer meeting again!" But that's just because of our false idea of what worship is. It is a circus! It is celebration, if the pictures in Revelation catch the flavor.

My daughter Ann heard her brother practicing the 23rd Psalm for his kindergarten graduation when she was about four. After he'd finished the words, *"And I will dwell in the house of the Lord forever"*, she said, "But, Mama, can't you never go outdoors?" In the sunny climate of constant praise of God there's "no need of moon nor stars by night, nor sun to shine by day." If we want to be at home up there, we'd better get used to it here.

Who are these clothed in white robes? The elder said, *"These are they who have come out of the great tribulation."* These are they who have passed through the great ordeal. These words were originally written to people who lived daily under the threat of extermination by the power of the state. They lived

---

[4] Ephesians 2:3-10
[5] Revelation 7:15

in a time when a throne threatened them, the throne of Caesar. They looked forward to a time when a throne would protect them... when he who sat upon the throne would, "*shelter them with his presence,*" because they had come through persecution and martyrdom in a hostile Roman Empire. But for us the words still ring true. There are modern equivalents of martyrdom.

A mother of children abandoned by a husband, because our laws now allow no-fault divorce, faces 73% less income typically than she enjoyed before, while her husband enjoys 42% more personal, disposable income. She has no really marketable skills if she's the average, but the law now judges them equal. If she makes it and rears those children without losing her faith, she has gone through the great tribulation, and there's a robe waiting for her.

Once a group of martyrs arrived at the entrance of the beloved country. The guardian of the gate said to them: "God has given much to you. Have you brought any gift for him?"

The martyrs said, "Only our pain, and that is nothing compared with Christ's suffering for us."

But the guardian said, "Even so, it is a good gift, and you are doubly welcome as comrades of the cross."

Who are these clothed in white robes? According to the elder, they are those who are shepherded by the Lamb. *"For the Lamb in the midst of the throne will be their shepherd, and he will guide them to springs of living water."*[6] What a striking figure! What is this? A tender, gentle, little lamb as their shepherd? A lamb leading and guiding the old ram-tough, competing males and the nurturing ewes? It seems a reversal of nature. But the final robe-wearers will be sheep who belong to the shepherd who is the Lamb of God.

Jesus makes this clear in the gospel reading. (John 10:24-27) Some people are having a hard time believing that he is the Christ, that he is the shepherd, and he says, *"You do not*

---

[6] Revelation 7:17

believe, because you do not belong to my sheep. My sheep hear my voice, and I know them and they follow me."

As the great patriarch, Chrysostom, put it, "They do not believe, not because Jesus is not a shepherd, but because they are not sheep." To be qualified to wear the white robe involves a leap of faith, a placing of yourself in the flock. Faith is a possibility for those who will to do the will of God. For those who stand back, arms folded, waiting to be convinced, final proof is never enough. Those who voluntarily enter the flock hear the shepherd's voice, and they're the only ones who know he is the shepherd. So come on in to the fold. Be a part of the flock. Be guided by the Lamb who is the shepherd. That's the necessary minimum.

A little boy was asked to give his favorite Bible verse. He said, "The Lord is my shepherd. That's all I want!" And that's all you need. Do we know him as shepherd?

Joe Cannon of Blakely spoke on laity Sunday at one of my churches several years ago and used the old story about the actor and the preacher. I saved it for later use. You've probably heard it because in recent years I've seen it circulating on the Internet. But ever since I was pastor out at Laurel Branch right after I retired, in my mind, the principal characters are the great actor, Charlton Heston, and Glen Kiser. Glen Kiser was the beloved pastor of Laurel Branch who served twenty-eight years out there before he died.

Charlton Heston, who has recorded much of the Bible on tape, was asked to give one of his favorite readings to the crowd assembled on Homecoming at Laurel Branch. Since he was not only an actor, but also President of the National Rifle Association at the time, he was in Macon campaigning for George Bush for President. (Don't be so skeptical. It could have happened!)

So Heston stood and recited the 23rd Psalm with his mellifluous voice in perfectly rounded tones. It was a masterpiece of recitation and when he finished the people applauded loudly.

But Brother Kiser was there and somebody who loved him suggested that he, too, be asked to recite the 23rd Psalm to close the morning service. Very reluctantly, he was ushered to the pulpit, and after much persuasion, he began in a much worn voice to recite the beloved words, "*The Lord is my shepherd, I shall not want.*" When he finished, there was no applause. Instead there was a holy hush over the crowd while here and there a tear quietly trickled down a cheek. The pastor had to break the silence and call for a blessing for the Homecoming dinner to get anybody to move toward the social hall.

Later, at the meal, somebody said, "Mr. Heston, why was it that when you recited the Psalm the people applauded, but when Brother Kiser recited it, they only became hushed and reverent?"

Heston said, "Well, I guess it's that they could tell that **I** know the 23rd Psalm, but **he** knows the shepherd."

Who are these clothed in white robes? Jesus said, "*My sheep hear my voice, and I know them, and they follow me.*"

ABOUT AMAZING GRACE
Romans 3:9-12, 21-24, Hebrews 13:9b

A man was out surveying his timber one afternoon when from deep within the forest he heard:
> Amazing Grace, how sweet the sound
> That saved a wretch like me.
> I once was lost, but now am found,
> Was blind but now I see.[1]

He made his way through the underbrush until he located the source. It was his woodcutter, John, chopping away at a log with all his might and singing at the top of his voice... "Amazing Grace!" The man stopped him, "John, do you believe in that grace that you're singing about so mightily?"

The answer came, "No-Sir, Mr. Robert, I was just singing."[2]

In our churches we do a lot of singing about grace. "God of Grace and God of Glory," "Amazing Grace," "Come Thou Fount of Every Blessing, Tune my heart to sing Thy Grace." Could it be that we, too, are just singing? You might think so at first merely from the fact that grace is such a shopworn word. It's a word in our day that has so many meanings that its crucial Christian meaning might be lost. We speak of having "grace" at meals. The bird in its flight is graceful, indicating a smooth symmetry of motion. The insurance company gives you a period of grace to pay the premium and we appreciate that. Although grace is always a lovely word, it could nevertheless easily lose its meaning, from its wide and indiscriminate use. However, it is my conviction that the Christian Church has not lost the meaning of grace entirely. When we sing about grace we are not just singing. When we sing about grace we're singing about the heart of the good news of the gospel.

---

[1] John Newton, 1779, No. 378 The Methodist Hymnal
[2] Rev. J. P. Dell, Annual Conference SGC, 1959

When we sing about grace we sing about the Father's infinite forgiveness. Here it: is in the scripture..."*Let us come boldly unto the throne of grace that we may obtain mercy.*"[3] And here it is in song:

> God's love, his mercy, and his grace
> combine to raise a fallen race;
> his hand is ready ere we call,
> held out with forgiveness for all.[4]

It doesn't take but a moment more to remember having seen it in life, for on life's. every day level God's grace functions as forgiveness. Although it cost him the death of his son, since that gift has already been given, I sometimes think that God must enjoy the business of being God more when his grace is busy forgiving sinners than when he is doing all the many other things God has to do.

During the First World War a story came out about a mother whose unusually brilliant son gave his life on the battlefront. He was a genius and had flowered early. From the first he had led his classes, and at Oxford he went on to win distinct honors. But he went to war, and an exploding shell blotted out his life. The mother dreamed a singular dream. She thought an angel came and told her she could have her son back for five minutes. The angel said, "Choose what five minutes you will have. Will you have five minutes of his life when he was leading classes at Oxford? Or would you prefer to have five minutes of those days that he spent in the service of his country, those last days of his life?"

The mother thought for a moment. "If I can have him back for five minutes, I should prefer to have him, not as an Oxford Student, nor during his soldier days. If I can have him but five minutes, I want to have him as a little boy on a day he disobeyed me. I remember how he ran into the garden, angry and rebellious. Then in a little while he came back and threw himself into my arms, asking me to forgive him. His face was

[3] Hebrews 4:16
[4] Cokesbury Hymnal No. 153,

hot and red. He looked so small and miserable, and so precious. I saw his love in his eyes. I felt his love in his body pressed against my own. And how my love went out to him! If I can have him back but five minutes, I want to take him back as that little penitent boy."[5]

Oh we have to come and ask for his grace if it's to function as forgiveness. *"The hard and impenitent heart only treasures up wrath for itself."*[6] Accepting no grace we reap what we sow. But his grace is there and we sing about it.

So let us come boldly unto the throne of grace, that we may obtain mercy—the Father's Infinite Forgiveness. Truly, *"it is a good thing that the heart be established with grace"*.

When we sing about grace we also sing about the solution for the separation of sin. Here we sing,

Grace, Grace, God's Grace,
Grace that will pardon and cleanse within.
Grace, Grace, God's Grace,
Grace that is greater than all our sin.[7]

It comes from the Scripture *"Where sin abounded, grace did much more abound."*[8] This means a little bit more than forgiveness only. Grace is the divine remedy that deals with the human disease called sin. I think we can relate this grace of God to our own experience when we think of sin as the opposite of grace. What is the opposite of grace? It's **dis**grace! Grace, then, is the cure for **dis**grace or the solution for the separation of sin.

We are disgraced whenever we are shut out or looked down on by a group or a town or a friend or members of our families. Whenever we have done something that has reflected on our families or our friends or our own best conscience we feel disgraced. There's a wall of separation between them and us. It can be just a minor thing that causes disgrace. You show

---

[5] Redhead, *Getting to Know God*
[6] Romans 2:5
[7] Julia H. Johnston, 1911 (Romans 5:20)
[8] Romans 5:20

up at a party in blue jeans. You thought it was a casual affair and you get there and everybody has on evening dress. You feel disgraced, shut out, different, separated. Or on a deeper level, through some behavior that's completely rejected by his town, someone has utterly disgraced the family. The father and mother are ashamed to go out and face their friends again. A great wall of separation stands between father or mother and child. So it is when we are in a state of sin. We are disgraced. We are shut out. We feel rejected by our former friends, our deepest best self and our God.

Grace, then, is answer to the problem of sin or separation. It is a healing of the hurt of disgrace. It is reunion. Grace is the conquering something that restores a broken relationship. At the party, grace is the kind person who speaks a word or offers a dress to the one in blue jeans to make them feel at home. In the family, it's the mother going to the daughter or the father going to the son to say, "This thing is done now and our home is open to you as always. Let's make the best of it together." Such a sharing of the hurt of disgrace and a healing of the separation of sin was done when God sent his only son who suffered because of our sins. And, if we accept this grace and go back into the father's house, that's reunion isn't it? Grace is a crossing of the gulf of separation between God and us and let's under-score the word "cross." Christ on the cross becomes the bridge over which we walk to make our way back into the father's house. And "*We... rejoice in God through our Lord Jesus Christ through whom we have now received our reconciliation.*"[9]

But you say, with such a good cure for sin as grace why don't we just stay in our sinful condition or sin some more. God's grace is there to restore the broken relationship. Paul answers this for us. "*Are we to continue in sin that Grace may abound? God forbid!*" If you go back into the father's house you're going to live like his child aren't you? If you are really

---

[9] Romans 5:11

re-united with him, you're not going to act like you're
separated are you? You don't want to cause him to suffer
again, do you? No! When you accept his grace you say to God,
"Be of sin the double cure,
Save from wrath and make me pure."[10]
When we sing about grace, we sing about the solution for the
separation of sin. God conquers the broken relationship, cures
our sin and disgrace. *"Where sin abounded, Grace did much more
abound."* Yes! *"It is a good thing that the heart be established with
grace." [11]*

Then when we sing about grace we sing about getting
something for nothing. *"Since all have sinned: and fall short of the
glory of God, they are justified by his grace as a gift."* Moffatt and
Goodspeed translate it, *"They are justified by his grace for
nothing.[12]"* In the hymn we sing it,
In my hands no price I bring,
Simply to Thy cross I cling.
Now how many places in this world today can you get
something for nothing? It's against all the rules of life. We
teach our children, "Don't expect to get something for
nothing, Son." You certainly can't get "something for
nothing" in the markets of this world, in the stores, or on the
job or even in the church. In fact, as many of you would
witness, the church is one of the most costly places you can
go. My brother in law used to say, "Salvation may be as free as
water, but just like with water, you sure do have to pay to get
it piped to you." He said that in their Primitive Baptist church
they do have some members that come to church singing, "In
my hands no price I bring," but they ought not to be singing
it. He said, "They ought to be giving their share like the rest of
us."

---

[10] Augustus M. Toplady, 1776, No. 361 United Methodist Hymnal
[11] Reasoning in this section from Wedel, *The Pulpit Rediscovers
Theology,* pp. 90-105
[12] Romans 6:1

The one place we get something for nothing is at the throne of God's Grace. In the third chapter of Romans, Paul gives one of the most sweeping indictments ever drawn up against the human race. *"None is righteous... the throat is an open grave, full of venomous lies... shedders of blood... no fear of God."* To greater or lesser degrees, all have sinned. None of us has a leg to stand on in the presence of God. Now for the sentence— *"Justified by his grace as a gift."* If God were a bookkeeper, this kind of bookkeeping would be the despair of a Certified Public Accountant. Look at all the debits and no credits. And God cancels the debt as a gift? It doesn't seem fair or right really. But we miss the point when we make God out to be a bookkeeper.

A Husband has been unfaithful to his wife and she knows it. But the husband has now found his new relationship to have but a passing joy and he feels guilty about it. He wants to regain his former relationship with his wife. He knows that there is this wall of separation between them because of his behavior and so he tries to think of some way to overcome it. On the way home he notices the flower shop and he thinks, "I'll get her an orchid, or a dozen roses." He buys them and goes home with his flowers. He doesn't confess to her his unfaithfulness. He sticks the orchid out. "I got this for you honey. Thought you might like to wear it to church tomorrow." She freezes and shoves the flowers away, turns, runs, slams the bedroom door and falls across the bed weeping. He stomps out of the house having failed in his attempt to make propitiation for his sins. He then tries candy, he tries clothes; he tries giving other gifts to bridge the gap between them.

Finally he realizes that none of this is of any avail in restoring the relationship. The sobering truth finally settles in upon him that if they are to get back together it will be because **she** makes the gift. The reconciling act must come from the wife; as sheer gift, sheer grace. Nothing that he can buy for her or do for her can overcome that vast chasm that separates them. And so one night, without making any purchases in any flower shops, he goes to his house; he makes his wife listen to him; he begs her forgiveness and the chance for a new life with her, and in effect says,

> "In my hands no price I bring,
> Simply to thy cross I cling."

With the marks of the suffering she has been through upon her face, her heart melts and she opens her arms to receive him. This is getting something for nothing. Her forgiveness has to be a gift.

But now it is that the flower shop really comes into its own. The forgiven husband rushes back and practically buys out the whole place to shower his wife with flowers, but now his acts are not in an attempt to buy his way into his wife's favor. They are the result of the surge of gratitude he feels for grace.

So it is between God and us. Our sin separates us. We try to win our way back into favor by righteous acts until we realize that the gift must come from God. We can't make propitiation ourselves. *"If any one sins, we have an advocate with the father; Jesus Christ the righteous, and he is the propitiation for our sins."[13]* Christ is the one that restores the relationship and he came from God. All we can do is accept the gift by faith, and then it is that we can truly do good works for him. A verse in Ephesians keeps this order of things right. *"By grace are ye saved through faith... unto good works."[14]* We have to accept something for nothing before we can do anything that counts with God. *"Truly it is a good thing that the heart be established with grace."*

Then when we sing about grace, we sing about the most charming characteristic of a Christian. Grace is not only something we receive as a gift, it is something that we show outward toward others. Peter says, *"As every one hath received the*

---

[13] I John 2:1-2
[14] Ephesians 2:8-10

gift, even so minister the same one to another, as good stewards of the manifold grace of God."[15] In the church we have talked a lot about the stewardship of money, but we haven't talked enough about the stewardship of grace. Christians are stewards of grace. And how the world is crying out for the grace that we are supposed to show forth!

> Down in the human heart,
> crushed by the tempter,
> Feelings lie buried that
> Grace can restore.
> Touched by a loving heart,
> wakened by kindness,
> Chords that were broken
> will vibrate once more. [16]

How we need to *"grow in the grace of our Lord and Savior Jesus Christ, who was full of grace and truth."*[17] Grace is the loveliest flower that can grow in the garden of the Christian's heart. A Christian is a gracious person... one who restores broken relationships.

When I first started out in the ministry I served among a people who did not have the same views on race that I held. At the time it was a very hot issue and at a youth meeting following church one night I gave rather radical expression to some of my ideas. At least it seemed radical for that time— 1953. When we were driving home in the car, Day said, "You're going to hear from that meeting." Worse luck you know, these wives are sometimes right.

By the next morning, two or three men of the church were incensed at me, and by ten o'clock I was called on the carpet in the chief preacher's office. Using all the language permissible to a preacher, and some that I didn't think was so permissible; he proceeded to take me apart. He told me how

[15] I Peter 4:10
[16] Fanny J. Crosby, 1869, 591 *United Methodist Hymnal*
[17] II Peter 3:18

these men were angry and he didn't have to tell me about his rejection of me. He sent me from there to see the Chairman of the Board. He was a lawyer whom I knew as a man who could use his tongue and I went trembling and knocked gingerly on his office door. I went in and he smiled at me. I was amazed. I expected to be raked over the coals. But the gist of what he said to me was this. "Hamp, you have seen the effect of the radical way you expressed yourself in the life of this church. I think you know the harm you've done. Let that be your only punishment as far as I'm concerned. I personally respect your freedom of opinion as a person and especially as a minister and I would die for your right to preach what you believe."

We shook hands; I mean really shook, for mine was shaking with gratitude. I left the office and ever since that day I've been searching for someone to whom I can show that same kind of grace. *"While we were yet sinners Christ died for us." "As every one hath received the gift, even so minister the same one to another, as good stewards of the manifold grace of God."*

Could we know the grace of God in his forgiveness and be reunited with him accepting his gift? Could we grow the grace of God in the garden of our own hearts? Could we show the grace of God to restore the broken relationships of our day? It would be good if we could, *"For it is a good thing that the heart be established with grace."*

THE MAIN THING AS THE MAIN THING
Matthew 28:16-20, Luke 13:29-30

Now the eleven disciples went to Galilee, to the mountain to which Jesus had directed them. When they saw him, they worshiped him; but some doubted. And Jesus came and said to them, 'All authority in heaven and on earth has been given to me. Go therefore and make disciples of all nations, baptizing them in the name of the Father and of the Son and of the Holy Spirit, and teaching them to obey everything that I have commanded you. And remember, I am with you always, to the end of the age.'

Then people will come from east and west, from north and south, and will eat in the kingdom of God. Indeed, some are last who will be first, and some are first who will be last.

Dr. Harry Denman, who had been a great layman in First Methodist Church of Birmingham, Alabama, became head of our Board of Evangelism back in the 1940's through 60's. As the visiting evangelist, he was preaching in Unadilla, Georgia, several years ago. While they were on their way to the little drug store in town for a soda, he suggested to the host pastor that they visit prospects for the church. The preacher said, "Oh we don't have any prospects for church membership here. Everybody in this little town belongs to some church already."

When they went in the drug store, Dr. Denman spotted a teen-aged boy near the soda fountain, and said to him. "Can I buy you a Coke?"

The boy said, "Sure."

Denman said, "Son, where do you go to church?"

The boy said, "I don't go!"

Denman said, "Well, are you a member of any church?"

The boy said, "No, sir!"

Dr. Denman turned to the host pastor and said, "Here's one."

So all around us, no matter where we are, there are persons who need to become disciples of Jesus Christ.

The *Discipline* of the United Methodist Church opens the section called "The Ministry of All Christians" by saying— "The mission of the Church is to make disciples of Jesus Christ." It's easy to see where we got that, if we just refresh ourselves on the Gospel reading for today. Jesus says, "*Go therefore and make disciples.*" In recent years, the hierarchy of the Church and the leadership of our Annual Conference have been saying that we all need to really focus on this. They say that we need to "Make the main thing the main thing."

But what is meant by that? What about this other little saying of Jesus: *Then people will come from east and west, from north and south, and will eat in the kingdom of God. Indeed, some are last who will be first, and some are first who will be last.*

Oh we have to make the main thing the main thing by making disciples of Jesus Christ. But I've been concerned across the years of this emphasis that some of those making the loudest noises and pushing for evangelism the strongest, really have no idea what they are pushing for if it were to come to pass.

My mother came to Baxley, Georgia from her home in Talbot County, Georgia, leading singing for Bishop Warren A. Candler as he preached a revival at Baxley, when she was twenty years of age. She wound up marrying my father, who was a forty-year-old bachelor lawyer in Baxley. She sang a solo that week:

> The Gospel Train is Comin'
> I hear it just at hand.
> Get on board, little children!
> There's room for many a more![1]

---

[1] Spiritual-From: Guitar Picker (www.gospelmusic.tk)

That leads me to say that though it saddened me and broke my heart, as it always does when anyone breaks the fellowship, I really considered it sort of a compliment to our church at Wesley Monumental in Savannah when I got a letter from a member withdrawing membership. The letter said, "Your church is too all-inclusive." I don't know whether this was referring to the fact that all kinds of persons of all races, genders, and lifestyles were welcome to worship there. It could have been that. Or it could have been the fact that our Wesley Gardens facilities on Moon River had been recently shared by our youth with the racially mixed children of the homeless. Whatever the reason, we weren't going to change those tentative efforts to reach out to others, for we were a long way yet from being patterned and programmed like the kingdom.

Making the main thing the main thing! Does that mean that we're to concentrate on individual conversion and adding people to church rolls to the exclusion of other values that are implicit in Jesus' charge to his disciples?

When he was in college at Emory University, Sammy Clark said, "My roommate's name was Fleetwood Maddox." I think Fleetwood is an old Macon boy.

Sammy said, "There were two slots for names on the dormitory door, but I had not bothered to put my own name up. I was studying, but Fleetwood was in Chemistry lab. Two seminary students came in the open door and said that they were concerned about the fact that most Emory freshmen did not have a personal experience with Jesus. Then they launched in with their 'evangelism?'

They asked if they could pray with me. They had already asked me if I were saved, and when I told them that I was a Christian, they told me that being a church member was not enough, that I needed a personal relationship with Christ. Then they prayed, 'Lord help Fleetwood see the light. Lord please send your Spirit into Fleetwood.' And on and on.

When they finished the prayer, they wished me well and left the room. When Fleetwood came in, I told him he'd been prayed for. I couldn't get over the fact that they never even asked me my name."

Is that making the main thing the main thing? Or were these would-be Christians just carrying out what they thought their job was as Christians, maybe to make some points for themselves with God. How easy it is to let the main thing get lost in the shuffle.

Sometimes I think it's kind of like the difference between the second stanza and the third stanza of that old hymn, *Rescue the Perishing*. The second stanza says, "Rescue the perishing, duty demands it." Is that why we should be winning disciples? Duty demands it? I like the third stanza better:

> "Down in the human heart,
> crushed by the tempter,
> Feelings lie buried that grace can restore.
> Touched by a loving heart,
> wakened by kindness,
> Chords that were broken
> will vibrate once more."

I believe that's the way Mrs. Lela Robitsch saw it. I was concerned for the survival of her little church. It only had thirty members, and a third of them lived in a big town ten miles from the church. But, you know, I don't think she even thought about that. She was a dumpy, little, older woman who lived near the church but knew about a beautiful, young wife who lived three miles north of the church. She knew this lovely Catherine was pretty miserable, wanting children, unable to have any, and married into a situation that required her to keep shifting her living arrangements every other week to go up the road and give live-in care to her husband's aging father.

Lela started going to see her just to cheer her up. She was the kind of lady who saw humor in every situation, and she helped Catherine to see some humor even in hers. That summer, the little church had its Vacation Bible School. It didn't have many children of its own, but staged it for the community. Lela thought to ask Catherine to pick up five or six children that lived up her road and bring them. When the annual revival was held, Lela invited Catherine. On the last verse of the last hymn, Catherine walked the aisle and joined the church. She was out of a tradition that wanted baptism by immersion, so I had to borrow a Baptist pool and immerse her. It was my first experience at doing this, and if Catherine hadn't seen it done before, we both would have drowned. Lela laughed at both of us.

When I think about making disciples of Jesus Christ, I might think of a long-term Bible study that requires lots of reading and hours of discussion. I might think of scripture memorization, extended periods of prayer, or going from door to door witnessing to strangers. I might think analytically; discipleship is about following someone. A disciple is someone who learns a way of living by following someone else. In this case it's learning to follow Jesus. I might think all of these things.[2] But if I really want to remember how to make the main thing the main thing, all I have to do is get a picture in my mind of a dumpy, little, loving lady with a laugh.

A few months later, Lela took sick and died and the sound of her laughter was heard in the church no more. But if we could be quiet enough, I think we could still hear her chuckle as Catherine left her home to pick up the children on her road and carry them to a Sunday-school class. We might hear her laugh out loud or even shout, because the once lonely Catherine has become the smiling Christian witness that she is.

Is that making the main thing the main thing?

---

[2] Thoughts of Ashley Randall, Rincon United Methodist Church Bulletin front c. 2005

REACHING UP OUT OF DARKNESS
For An Anniversary of 9/11

Psalm 42

As a deer longs for flowing streams, so my soul longs for you, O God. My soul thirsts for God, for the living God. When shall I come and behold the face of God? These things I remember, as I pour out my soul: how I went with the throng, and led them in procession to the house of God, with glad shouts and songs of thanksgiving, a multitude keeping festival. Why are you cast down, O my soul, and why are you disquieted within me? Hope in God; for I shall again praise him, my help and my God. My soul is cast down within me; therefore I remember you from the land of Jordan and of Hermon, from Mount Mizar. Deep calls to deep at the thunder of your cataracts; all your waves and your billows have gone over me. By day the LORD commands his steadfast love, and at night his song is with me, a prayer to the God of my life. I say to God, my rock, "Why have you forgotten me? Why must I walk about mournfully because the enemy oppresses me?" As with a deadly wound in my body, my adversaries taunt me, while they say to me continually, "Where is your God?" Why are you cast down, O my soul, and why are you disquieted within me? Hope in God, for I shall again praise him, my help and my God.

How do you begin a sermon on the anniversary of 9/11? We don't know who the psalmist was, but he surely could have been speaking for all of the relatives of those lost on that fateful day... *I say to God, my rock, "Why have you forgotten me? Why must I walk about mournfully because the enemy oppresses me?"* Remembering those lost... conscious of the enemy still out there. He says, *My tears have been my food day and night, while people say to me continually, "Where is your God?"* My tears have been my food day and night? That's quite a diet. You could probably reduce faster on that than you could on a Medithin program

The psalmist is probably an exile in Babylon, modern Iraq today, who has seen his family destroyed as he was carried off into captivity and exile. An old song goes, "None but the lonely heart can know my sorrow." He says, *Deep calls to deep at the thunder of your cataracts.* It's his poetic way of saying, "Out of the deep, to which I have gone down, lift me up."

Apart from 9/11, many people today feel this way. I was in a Counseling Training Course in which we pastors were asked to bring in sample counseling kits filled out. We just got chance candidates from our churches to fill them out. But we brought in reports that indicated people feel they are down in darkness, in a pit from which they can't extricate themselves. We're beginning to feel this way about our involvement in Iraq.

As I study this dilemma, I think I understand how Mark Twain felt in his story, *"The Terrible Medieval Tragedy."* He had developed a situation to the point where every single character in the story was going to be destroyed as a result of any conceivable move that would be made by the principal agents. Having done this, Mark Twain closes the story by saying, "I have these characters in such a fix I cannot get them out. Anyone who thinks he can is welcome to try!"

But as I was researching this psalm, I found out that the Interpreter's Bible called it, "The Despair and Hope of a Godly Person." Did you notice how this very religious, godly person alternates between despair and hope? He says, *Why are you cast down, O my soul, and why are you disquieted within me? Hope in God, for I shall again praise him, my help and my God.*

At the entrance to the building of The League of Nations, there is a figure over the door of a man reaching his hand up into the heights to touch a hand that is reaching down out of the mist. Underneath is this inscription: "Lord of the living and the dead, I feel thy hand and find Thee."

Out of the darkness a hand reaches up to grab hold of the sustaining power of memory. *"These things I remember as I pour out my soul."* He remembers the faith of all those at the temple and his own joy in it. The Psalmist, whether a leader or just one of the crowd, loved to join with the pilgrim processions, the multitudes keeping festival; the memory of the past revives his languishing soul. He was one who had stored up in his life great affirmations of faith that would do in times of crisis. How much better shape was he in than some today whose only memories of Sunday would be how many fish they caught or how many miles they drove.

At funerals sometimes I use the scripture: (Lamentations) *"Jerusalem remembers in the days of her affliction and bitterness all the precious things that were hers from days of old."* The Jews were able to rebuild their temple and their faith on the basis of memory. So long as something is in the memory, it can't be taken away. We can rebuild and add to it. So crisis can come, but with the power of memory we can recover and add a brick or two to our life structure, gained from this experience.

Perhaps Colleen Kelly says it best. Colleen, the bereaved sister of Billy Kelly, who was struck down that day at the WTC, has become a world activist for restorative justice through the group she has co-founded, 9/11 Families for Peaceful Tomorrows. She speaks for so many of us when she says that, as strange as it may sound, she is a more hopeful person since September 11, and believes this act has the potential to "lead to so much greater good... I still believe that good will overcome, that goodness will overcome, and that my worldview has not been shattered. There were too many good things that happened that day, and all the days afterward - the thousands and thousands and thousands of acts of kindness. If anything, I am more firm in my belief in God; more firm in my belief in family; more firm in my belief that there is an overwhelming goodness in the world, and that goodness will overcome."[1]

Many of us know that's it's good to have an objective view of the self. During a revival meeting, the eloquence of the evangelist brought a listener to his feet. "Brethren," he

---

[1] PBS Online, *Memories of 9/11*

declared, "I've been a sinner, a contemptible sinner. And I've been one for years... but I never knew it before tonight!"

"Sit down; brother," whispered the deacon stationed in the aisle. "The rest of us knew it all the time!" With an objectivity of mind, this man might have known it first himself.

And it's valuable in other ways. Our Psalmist doesn't completely despair, for out of the darkness, his hand reaches up to find this objectivity of mind. He was able to reason with himself as though **he** was not personally involved. He spoke to himself as if he were another person. He says, *"Why are you cast down, O my soul, and why are you disquieted within me?"* I heard Gaston Foote say that one of the most encouraging verses in the Bible was one that is repeated hundreds of times: *"It came to pass."* Think about this verse when you meet the hard things in life... *It came to pass.* It didn't come to stay. This is what the Psalmist is saying to himself.

"I said to myself" is a practical device, and who doesn't accept it and practice it at times. It's self-communion by way of introspection, and when it is free from being morbid and self-centered, it is one of the most useful disciplines of personal religion. How valuable if we can get sufficiently removed from our own personal hurt and trouble to speak to ourselves as we have probably reasoned to others in trouble. God will help; time will help; the loved one will be better off than they would have been suffering. All these things that are no help from another could register if we tell them to ourselves. How much more quickly could we move out of despair if we could get the unemotional objective perspective of another person on our problems.

This Psalmist doesn't completely despair because out of the darkness a hand reaches up to grasp an unquenchable consciousness of God. Whether it is day or night, he is conscious of God. *"By day the Lord commands his steadfast love; and at night his song is with me."* The Psalmist has a **normal** religious experience; he has ups and downs in his religious experience. But the central thing is that whatever the feeling is, it brings a consciousness of God. Many make the mistake of believing that religion must always enable us to present a bright face; we must have a radiant countenance. If we are crushed by crisis, then there must be some weakness to our faith. Like the woman that came up to Fred Craddock's sister at the funeral home, right after she had lost her husband and said, "Aren't you just thrilled beyond words that your husband has gone to be with God?" How fakey is that?

This Psalm tells us that the godly person can go through a period of despair, which is real, and then have hope in the midst of despair. *"As a hart longs for flowing streams, so longs my soul for thee, O God."* The figure is that of an animal of the chase, parched with thirst and panting for the one source of relief, the cool, fresh water of ever running streams. His very situation of need makes him long for God. *"I need thee every hour."* Some would curse, but this man longs for God when he gets in deep trouble. An old Negro man was in a North Carolina hospital just before his leg was to be cut off. He said to his pastor, Wilson Weldon, "I ain't afraid; I got my Jesus right here."

It is by maintaining the tension between the alternate moods of the spirit that the spirit stays vital. To go without any water is to die of thirst. To abandon oneself to the water-brook is to drown in it. To know deeply that we are by our very nature ordained to move in the cadence of joy and sorrow, fulfillment, and dismay; and to use each mood as the Psalmist has done, to call the heart back to the awareness of God... this is truly to live in the Divine Presence.

In Sammy Clark's Inner City Church in Savannah, in one of their afternoon Bible Study sessions with teenagers, Sammy asked them, "Why were Paul and Silas singing in prison?"

One of the boys whose only experience of singing in prison was telling on your companions in crime in order to plea-bargain said, "Because they wanted to get out."

Sammy had to point out, "No, they were singing because they had this unquenchable consciousness of God."

The Rev. Lyndon Harris, Priest-in-Charge, St. Paul's Chapel, New York, that's right across the street from where the World Trade Center went down on 9/11, had a faithful fireman in his church. He says, "We were across the street from J & R Music World, and he took me over to a tree and showed me all kinds of boots in the tree. He specifically wanted me to go over and see those boots. He said, "Do you know the story of these boots?"

And I said, "No, tell me about them."

With tears in his eyes he said, "These are the boots of people who came in the first wave to help out. They didn't have the luxury of changing in the firehouse like I did. They had to get changed on the way."

There were mountain-climbing boots, work boots. There was even a pair of high heels. All kinds of shoes. All kinds of boots. And he said, "These guys had to change when they got here. And because they were in the first wave, they won't be coming back for their boots."

That's the despair of even the godly person as we go through the darkness of this life. But out of the darkness our hands can reach up to lay hold on the sustaining power of memory, an objectivity of mind, and an unquenchable consciousness of God. They may not be coming back for their boots, but if we're quiet enough, we just might be able to hear like an echo from another world:

> I gotta shoes; you gotta shoes!
> All o' God's chillun gotta shoes!
> When I get to heaven, gonna put on my shoes
> Gonna walk all over God's heaven![2]

Merciful God, we pray for all who died in the tragedy of 9/11. We pray for those who survived, those who grieve, those who serve this land and this whole world of need and even for those who brought it about. And we pray that in time, out of the grief and the wreckage, your new creation may truly emerge. Amen.

[2] African American Spiritual

[3] Adapted from a prayer on PBS Online, *Remembering 9/11*

THE PATHWAY INTO
THE PEACE OF GOD
Acts 16:25-34[1]

O ne of the elusive quests of this nervewracked, distraught generation has been for peace of mind, peace of soul, peace of heart... if you will... peace of God. Paul once wrote the church at Philippi, and he said, *"And the peace of God which passes all understanding, will guard your hearts and minds through Christ Jesus."*[2] There must have been people in the Philippian church who had found the pathway into the peace of God for Paul to so confidently assure them that the peace of God would keep their hearts and minds. One among these was the jailer that we read about in Acts 16. What were the steps along the pathway into the peace of God for him?

First of all, he had an overpowering sense of personal need. He fell down before Paul and Silas and with fear and trembling in his voice he said, *"Sirs, what must I do to be saved?"*

This is the question that our generation is not asking, especially the "I." We don't understand anybody who thinks that **we** need to ask for salvation. Nobody says, "What must **I** do to be saved?"

> I fight alone, and win or sink,
> I need no one to make me free.
> I want no Jesus Christ to think
> That he could ever die for me.

But I think this is true. Until you've had an overpowering sense of personal need, you'll never have an overwhelming sense of personal victory. This is the kick-off in the game of

---

[1] You'll find this text in the King James Version at the close of this sermon.
[2] Philippians 4:7

faith and you'll never get the ball across the goal line until you've had it. You'll never have an overwhelming sense of personal victory until you've had an overpowering sense of personal need. Somewhere along the way you have to stop and ask, "What must **I** do?"

We were approaching Atlanta from the Northeast side coming beck from Lake Junaluska before the days of the freeway and I never had driven through that way before. Day said, "Hamp, are you sure you know the way through Atlanta this way?"

I said, "Honey, I didn't go to school in Atlanta four years for nothing. I know Atlanta like the back of my hand." But after I got into the city limits things began to look a little strange. If I knew Atlanta like the back of my hand, I began to realize that I never had looked too carefully at the back of my hand before. But, I wouldn't stop and ask anybody the way. So we wasted time twisting and turning in the thousand directions that Atlanta can lead you when you don't know your way. Do you know something? When you're lost and wasting time trying to find your way out of a strange city, you can be as lost as it's possible to be lost, but there's not a soul that's going to tell you how to find your way out until you ask them. And you can be so far from the peace of God that your life is tortured and tasteless. You can be worried about the smallest things. You can be so anxious that you can't sleep at night. You can be so far from the peace of God that you're living a hell on earth, but there's not a soul who is going to be able to point you to the pathway until you ask the way. Somewhere along the line you must have, or you must have had an overpowering sense of personal need. He said, "Sirs, what must **I** do to be saved?"

Then the jailer made a complete commitment to a personal Christ. This is what they told him he must do. He said, "What must I do:"

They said, "Believe on the lord Jesus Christ and you shall be saved." They asked him to make a committal of his heart and life to a person. I can believe in a person. I can have loyalty to a person. I can follow a person. I would have trouble and so would you if they had asked him to have a complete knowledge of the creeds of a church. I heard Dr. E. Stanley Jones say in a Revival at Statesboro, Georgia, that we often misunderstand this "Believe on the Lord Jesus Christ." He said it's not just an affirmation, a doctrinal acceptance that Christ is the way. He said it's more like an acrostic of the word "Faith." **F**-Forsaking... **A**-All... **I**-I ... **T**-Take... **H**- Him! Forsaking All I Take Him! It's a complete commitment to the person Jesus Christ and all he did and calls us to do. He was a person. His life was like ours. And he suffered as we suffer when we stand for right against the might of the world. We can commit our lives to the carpenter who went to a cross. We can take his hand unreservedly because in his hand there are both the calluses of the workingman and the nail-prints of the divine love.

On the way to peace we have tried everything else. Why not try this? We've tried to find peace by living in a particular place and discovered that it's not the place; it's the person. We've tried to find peace by drowning our devils in drink and we've discovered that the devils swim in it and thrive on it and become stronger. We've tried to find peace by getting for ourselves things and discovered that it's not the things a person has but the person who has the things that makes the difference. We've tried to find peace in place and poison and plenty and even sleeping pills and we're peace-less. Why don't we try this complete commitment to a personal Christ? For until we come through this commitment to the grace of God we have found only "cures that don't cure, blessings that don't bless and solutions that don't solve."[3]

---

[3] G. K. Chesterton

Then if the jailer is our guide along the pathway into the peace of God, it will lead us to make a definite decision to undo the wrong that we have done. The jailer *"took them the same hour of the night and washed their wounds."* He took immediate action to modify his past mistakes. This is naturally hard for us to do. When I was a little boy, Joan Wood hit me, so I hit Joan Wood in the head with my fist. She ran down the street crying and told her grandmother. Her grandmother made the wires sing as she talked on the phone to my mother and soon I was on my way down the street at the point of a paddle. My mother was walking right behind me. We walked up on the porch and Joan came out. Right beneath her blond curls there was an egg shining forth from her forehead where I had hit her. I was at that awkward age when you're too young to like girls. But her grandmother and my mother agreed that the proper resolution of this incident would be for me to apologize to Joan and kiss her to show that there were no hard feelings. Somehow I made it through it, but that's the poorest excuse for a kiss in the world—kissing a girl playmate when you're too young to like them and you're mad. It's naturally hard to make the decision to undo the wrong you've done. It doesn't just happen. But mark this; it always flows out of complete commitment to the person of Christ. If you really love as he loved, you're just as certainly forced into remedying the wrong you've done as I was at the point of that paddle. But you're not forced either. It's what you want to do. It's the most natural thing in the world to begin immediately to undo the wrong you've done. The jailer had inflicted the wounds, so he *"took them the same hour of the night and washed their wounds."*

What was it that Zaccheus said, *"Behold, half of my goods I give to the poor and If I have done aught against any man, I restore him four-fold."*[4] A definite decision to undo the wrong you've done! Of course, sometimes it's too late. Sometimes we can't bring

---

[4] Luke 19:1-10

back the past and redo it. Sometimes we must simply accept the forgiveness that comes with a complete commitment to Christ. But there has to be a definite decision to undo all the wrong that we **can** undo.

Baptism must have something to do with the next step along the pathway into the peace of God. Luke says, *"And he was baptized at once."* This may seem strange in a day when the ancient offices of the church are accorded so little significance. This may seem to some to even be a little bit narrow, but baptism in this case was the public expression of his inward intention. This is the natural outgrowth of a great commitment. This is true of anything to which you're truly committed. You're willing to let it be known. You remember when you met that little girl and fell in love with her. Before she became your wife, you had to stand up and publicly acknowledge that she was your whole life and love from that day on. It was a knee-shaking experience before God and everybody, but you were willing to do it, because you loved her. You had no fear of hypocrisy or failure, because you loved. You would never fail her and you'd tell the world so. In the same way, if you're truly committed to the personal Christ you'll tell the world so through baptism. You're willing to make the public expression of your inward intention. Oh I know baptism is more than this, but it is certainly the public expression of your inward intention. You can hardly do without it.

If you've had it, count it as a significant thing in your life. If you haven't had it, get baptized, because it's the natural outgrowth of a great commitment. It's a symbol of your overpowering sense of personal need before God. It's a symbol of your whole-hearted commitment to Christ. It's a symbol of your decision to undo the wrong you've done, and it's a symbol of the overflowing forgiveness of God for your life. It's a symbol of dying to sin and rising to new life in

Christ. It's a symbol that tells the world where you stand from now on. There's no question or worry about it. You're on the side of Christ. It will help bring peace.

What was the last step in this Scripture for this jailer along the pathway into the peace of God? The jailer *"Brought them up into his house, and set food before them; and he rejoiced with all his household that he had believed in God."* Could this be the church, the fellowship of the faithful, the supportive fellowship of the family of God? How would this help bring peace? Could it be that the church helps us to control our behavior making it more Christ-like? We don't have such a hard time living the Christian life. We don't "fight alone win or sink." We have Jesus Christ and our fellow Christians to help us. Your close companions' values help control the life you lead. And when the companionship is the fellowship of the church, Christian behavior is the natural result. The supportive fellowship of the family of God—if it's truly the church it supports you in *"love, joy, peace, patience, kindness, goodness, gentleness, faithfulness, self-control."*[5]

There are two phrases that I heard all of my boyhood at Baxley, Georgia, and I hope they've affected my life. When two men got together on the streets of Baxley and one would ask the other, "Who is that boy there yelling his head off selling newspapers?"

The other one would say, "Don't you know? That's Wade Watson's boy."

The second phrase always followed it. The other man would say, "You know, he was a fine man."

"Wade Watson's boy." "He was a fine man." I've been haunted by those phrases and with them the conviction that the least I could do was to try to live like the son of a fine man. I may not have always made it. But think what it can do

---

[5] Galatians 5:22

to your life when you firmly believe that you are a child of God, that your brothers and sisters in the church are brothers and sisters in Christ. Don't you think it would make it easier to shape your life after Him?

But I haven't yet mentioned the thing that many of you have already experienced for yourselves. You've discovered that the comfort afforded by that supportive fellowship can bring you to peace in time of grief quicker than any other force in the world. This isn't true of all companions when death strikes. Some of them will try to tell you that you have no right to grieve in spite of the fact that Jesus said, *"Blessed are they that mourn, for they shall be comforted."*[6] They will not know that you must mourn before the morning of peace comes. But there are those who *"are able to comfort those who are in any affliction, with the comfort with which they themselves are comforted by God."*[7]

I stood up with the congregation to recite the responsive reading, sing the *Gloria Patri* and then affirm *The Apostle's Creed.* But as a boy those phrases in the creed meant little to me: "I believe in the Holy Spirit, the holy catholic church, the communion of saints, the forgiveness of sins." That phrase, "The communion of saints"—what was that? Was that a reference to talking with the dead or having séances with ghosts? But when I became sixteen years of age I found out about the communion of the saints.

My pastor, Brother Ab Quillian, came to the classroom door at my High School and something in his manner made me get up from my seat and go to him. I knew before he told me that mother was dying in the hospital in Macon. We rode up there in virtual silence, one hundred and twenty miles, but

---

[6] Matthew 5:4
[7] II Corinthians 1:3-4

I felt that more went on between us than ever had in all the conversations I had ever had with him.

It was over in a day and we returned home. The folks started coming in at the house and the main ones I remember were the ones in the church. My close boy friends in the Sunday school class and MYF came and nervously shifted around, but before they left they hugged me or hit me on the shoulder. There was Mrs. Ira Leggett who had taught me in the Junior Class and given me my first Bible with my name on it in gold letters. There was Aleta, the organist, with whom I learned to sing my first songs of faith and by whose playing I led my first congregations in song. She didn't say a word. She just hugged me, but a depth of feeling passed between us that no words could capture. Later the flowers filled the church, and the preachers had to say something. But all the way through, you know what meant the most to me? It was the communion of the saints, the fellowship of the faithful, the supportive fellowship of the family of God. With their help, I found my way into some measure of peace.

Could we follow a jailer in the first century to peace? An overpowering sense of personal need, a complete commitment to a personal Christ, a definite decision to undo the wrong you've done, the outward expression of your inward intention and the supportive fellowship of the family of God—try these, and it may be you'll find *"the peace of God which passeth all understanding, shall keep your hearts and minds through Christ Jesus."*

Passage Acts 16:25-34:

And at midnight Paul and Silas prayed, and sang praises unto God: and the prisoners heard them. And suddenly there was a great earthquake, so that the foundations of the prison were shaken: and immediately all the doors were opened, and every one's bands were loosed. And the keeper of the prison awaking out of his sleep, and seeing the prison doors open, he drew out his sword, and would have killed himself, supposing that the prisoners had been fled. But Paul cried with a loud voice, saying, Do thyself no harm: for we are all here. Then he called for a light, and sprang in, and came trembling, and fell down before Paul and Silas, And brought them out, and said, Sirs, what must I do to be saved? And they said, Believe on the Lord Jesus Christ, and thou shalt be saved, and thy house. And they spake unto him the word of the Lord, and to all that were in his house. And he took them the same hour of the night, and washed their stripes; and was baptized, he and all his, straightway. And when he had brought them into his house, he set meat before them, and rejoiced, believing in God with all his house.